DIGITAL
ETIQUETTE

DIGITAL ETIQUETTE

VICTORIA TURK

EBURY
PRESS

3 5 7 9 10 8 6 4 2

Ebury Press, an imprint of Ebury Publishing,
20 Vauxhall Bridge Road,
London SW1V 2SA

Ebury Press is part of the Penguin Random House group of companies
whose addresses can be found at global.penguinrandomhouse.com

Penguin
Random House
UK

First published by Ebury Press in 2019

www.penguin.co.uk

A CIP catalogue record for this book is available from the British Library

ISBN 9781529102406

Printed and bound in Great Britain by Clays Ltd, Elcograf S.p.A.

Penguin Random House is committed to a
sustainable future for our business, our readers
and our planet. This book is made from Forest
Stewardship Council® certified paper.

CONTENTS

INTRODUCTION

O n the internet, no one knows you're a dog – but that's no excuse for poor manners.

Etiquette might sound like an old-fashioned idea in modern times, but it's about a lot more than knowing which fork to use. It is the social glue that binds us together, the code that lets us easily communicate without misunderstanding each other or causing offence. It helps us to avoid awkwardness and show respect to others, all while presenting ourselves in the best possible light.

But all too often, good manners seem to dissolve in the glare of a smartphone screen or the clicking of a keyboard. This isn't (usually) out of any malice; the problem is that there's very little consensus on what constitutes good conduct in the digital world. You might know your way around a dinner party, but how confident are you on the etiquette of WhatsApp groups? Does your Tinder profile meet generally accepted standards of decorum? And where does one even begin with social media? Any guidance on the correct usage of memes is conspicuously absent from my copy of Debrett's. . .

It's no wonder we're all confused. Behind our screens, communication is often conducted through text, meaning it doesn't benefit from social cues such as facial expressions and body language. Communication is rarely truly private, increasing the potential for embarrassment, and it almost always leaves a digital trail – all the better to capture a permanent record of your every indiscretion.

In the 1990s, people used to talk about 'netiquette' to describe a kind of general internet code of conduct. But as more and more of our interactions move online, we need more nuance. Context is critical: you wouldn't behave the same in an email to your boss as you would in a Snapchat message to your crush (or at least I hope you wouldn't). And as technology evolves, so too does our behaviour. Famed etiquette author Emily Post never had to consider how best to slide into someone's DMs, or deal with the exquisite agony of being left on read.

This book sets out to illuminate digital etiquette across the four major spheres of everyday life: work, romance, friendship and community. As well as offering practical advice, it reflects on some of the quirks of modern digital culture, and the behaviours we have developed to navigate these treacherous times. As technology moves on and customs change, it can be hard to keep up, but the basic pillars of good manners remain the same. Good etiquette means putting other people's comfort first. It means having empathy and patience, and generally just not being a jerk.

Keep these basic tenets in mind and we can bring ourselves one step closer to the impossible: being nice to each other on the internet.

PLEASE TAKE ME OFF THIS THREAD

THE ART OF WORK

FIVE GOLDEN RULES

1. Reduce email at all costs

2. An empty inbox is the path to enlightenment

3. Assume that everyone you email is smarter and busier than you

4. Reply-all at your peril

5. There is no excuse to leave a voicemail

We spend most of our waking hours at work and, in many workplaces, the majority of that time is spent staring at screens. One particular medium has come to dominate office communication: email. It's probably the first thing you check when you start your work day, and the last thing you do before you leave. It is the bane of the modern condition, and on that basis it is here that we shall begin our study of digital etiquette.

Things weren't always like this. Email has its roots way back before the internet as we know it, when American programmer Ray Tomlinson wrote some code that allowed users to send messages between computers on the ARPANET system (the precursor to today's internet) in the early 1970s. Tomlinson, who died in 2016, said he developed the system because it 'seemed like a neat idea' and maintained that the first emails he sent were so insignificant he had forgotten them.[1] I'm sure we can all relate.

It's undeniable that email has had a transformative effect on work culture. Without it, we'd never know the joy of working remotely, sharing ideas across continents, or passive-aggressively CCing the boss when dealing with an annoying colleague. But I think we can all agree that email is completely out of control. It no longer helps us do work; it *is* work. It may have freed us from the physical confines of the office, but mentally we can never leave. Email is distracting, time-consuming and intensely stressful.

This is where etiquette can help. The majority of the stress around email can be attributed to a lack of consensus on how to use it. How quickly must you respond to an email? How do you strike the right tone? And is there a law somewhere that says every message must begin 'Sorry for the late response'?

Together we shall dissect the ins-and-outs of proper email protocol, from subject line to sign-off. We shall resolve once and for all when email is the correct medium to use and consider alternative workplace communications such as conference calls, instant messaging tools and (steel yourself) LinkedIn. Once you're done with this chapter, just leave it lying conveniently open on the desk of that one person in the office who still hasn't got their head around the unwritten rules of reply-all.

Office email

The paradox of email is that it's simultaneously very convenient and utterly exhausting. It's often the most expedient way of getting things done, and yet it just seems to take up so much time.

If you're feeling the crunch, you're not alone. In one study presented at a conference in 2016, researchers asked 40 office workers to wear a heart rate monitor for 12 days and log their computer use during this time. The workers checked their email an average of 77 times a day and spent almost an hour and a half dealing with it. Sure enough, their heart data showed that the longer they spent on email within a given hour, the more stressed they were during that time. And the longer they spent on email each day, the less productive they felt they had been.[2]

Given that email is such a universal horror, good email etiquette really revolves around one thing: *reducing it as much as possible.* A considerate emailer strives to take up as little of their recipient's time and energy as they can. They email only when strictly necessary and take pains to make their messages as easy to deal with as possible. A considerate emailer understands that the best email is the one they don't actually send.

THE LIFE-CHANGING MAGIC OF TIDYING UP (YOUR INBOX)

B EFORE YOU CAN even think about sending emails to other people, you need to get your own house in order. After all, you can't hope to reduce the greater burden of email on the world if your own inbox is a digital dumping ground that threatens to engulf you with the next 'ping!' of a notification. And if you're barely treading water in a quicksand of unread messages, you could easily miss the one you actually need to respond to.

Do a quick internet search and you'll find that email management strategies are as abundant and diverse as fad diets – often with similarly unsatisfying results. There are entire self-help books dedicated to this topic, of which this is not one, so I'll cut to the chase and give you the only advice you need to bother with.

Sound too good to be true? Let me introduce you to Inbox Zero.

I am an Inbox Zero disciple. Those of us who have found inner inbox peace just can't stop ourselves from evangelising on the matter in an effort to save other poor souls from email purgatory. In my job as a magazine editor, I once found myself having to entertain a famous sports star ahead of a photo shoot. These forced moments of interaction are always stilted, and the conversation soon petered out into awkward silence – until:

'Have you heard about Inbox Zero?' I asked. (He had not, but I think I converted him.)

So what is Inbox Zero? The term was coined by blogger, podcaster and all-round productivity type Merlin Mann, who first laid out the strategy in several posts on his 43 Folders blog in 2006 and then in a Google Tech Talk in 2007. In these, Mann shares a simple way to triage your emails so they don't keep stacking up. Think of him like Japanese tidying-up guru Marie Kondo, except he's helping declutter your inbox instead of your sock drawer.

The driving idea of Inbox Zero is to keep your inbox empty by processing every email in some way as soon as you read it.

A few clarifications before you have a panic attack: this does not mean processing every email as soon as it *arrives,* nor does it mean *answering* every email. The point is that when you choose to read an email, you should do something with it, so that it doesn't just keep haunting your inbox, making you feel guilty. 'If I had to sum it up in one phrase, I would say that if you can find the time to check email, you must also use that time to do something with that email,' Mann tells me.

Still not convinced? Follow these three simple steps to embark on your own life-changing journey:

1. Start with a clean slate

Depending on your current email habits, this may require quite a brutal deep-clean. The sensible, grown-up way to do this would be to take some time to sit down and click through each unread message, deleting or responding as appropriate until you've cleared the decks. But let's be realistic. There's only really one thing for it: select-all + delete. Done.

If you struggle to let things go, you could move all of your unread emails into a separate folder to go through at a later date, or archive them instead. But if these emails have been kicking around unread for a while, it's unlikely they're that important – and if they are, people will find a way to contact you. They'll send another email. They'll mention it next time they see you. They'll call you on the phone (shudder).

Now, take a moment to revel in your new, squeaky-clean inbox. Congratulations, you have *no new emails*! Don't get too comfortable, however, because now the real work starts.

2. Turn off notifications

Or at least most of them. One reason email is the scourge of our working lives is that it's constantly distracting us from other things. You just get into your groove on a project and – ding! – your train of thought is rudely interrupted by Becky from finance, reminding you about the charity bake sale this afternoon. In one case study, researchers found that it took an average of 64 seconds for workers to get back on task after checking their email (and that's not including the time spent actually reading or dealing with the emails).[3] Check your inbox every ten minutes over an eight-hour stretch and that's 50 minutes of your working day spent just getting your head back into the zone after switching tasks.

Check your email on your own terms instead. Set your inbox to retrieve email at a specific interval rather than every time a new message arrives.

3. Only read each email once

Whenever you do check your inbox, the important thing is that you actually do something with the contents. As per Mann's mantra: 'Your job is not to read an email and then read it again.' Upon reading, he recommends immediately taking one of five actions: delete, delegate, respond, defer, do.

EXTRA EMAIL MANAGEMENT PRO-TIPS FOR THE TRUE INBOX NEAT-FREAK

Not got your fix? Keep your inbox spotless with these bonus techniques:

- Unsubscribe from all the newsletters you once enthusiastically signed up for but never actually read – these have a tendency to rapidly breed if left unsupervised.

- Set up automatic filters. Your email client probably already does this for spam, but you can set up your own rules to divert emails from certain senders or containing certain keywords straight to a designated folder, so they don't clog your inbox.

- Organise inbox folders by deadline, not subject. This way you can easily prioritise the emails you've deferred.

- Stop people emailing you in the first place by making your email address hard to find. Says Mann: 'Only an animal has their raw email address sitting out in public any more.'

The first one – 'delete' – is easy. If you have an email that is obviously rubbish, or that you don't need to do anything with after reading, then just get rid of it. Archive it instead of deleting if you want to keep it for reference purposes. 'Delegate' is also pretty simple: if it's someone else's concern, forward the email and be done with it. And 'respond' isn't as scary as it sounds. If an email requires a fast response, just do it.

Once you've completed these steps, you'll probably be surprised at how little remains. The remaining emails – the ones that actually require some real work – fall into the 'defer' and 'do' categories. Choosing when and how to 'defer' is the trickiest. Mann suggests moving deferred emails into a specific 'to do' folder so that you can keep track of them without clogging your main inbox. Just be mindful that you also work through that folder regularly; lingering emails are still lingering emails, regardless of how diligently you've filed them.

Put these points into practice and you'll wonder how you possibly managed before. Just one word of warning: it is possible to get a bit *too* carried away with keeping an empty inbox, to the point that it defeats the whole purpose of the exercise. After all, Mann says, 'The point of this is not to obsess about getting to zero. The point is to do less obsessing.'

When to send an email

It used to be that you'd leave your desk at 5 p.m. and would be uncontactable until 9 a.m. the next morning. Now that we're all carrying mini-computers in our pockets, however, there's a general assumption that we should all be digitally reachable at just a moment's notice.

But just because we *can* send emails at any time of the day or night doesn't mean we *should* (indeed, knowing the difference between 'can' and 'should' is pretty much the definition of good manners).

So insidiously has work email crept into our private lives that France has gone so far as to legislate against it, granting workers a 'right to disconnect' (*droit à la déconnexion*) that essentially enshrines in law a French employee's right to ignore their boss's emails and calls. The law, which was passed in 2017, doesn't dictate exactly how employers should restrict workers' use of digital tools but stipulates that companies should come up with a policy, agreed with employees, to limit digital encroachment into workers' personal and family lives. As I believe Robespierre once said: *Liberté, égalité, email-free.*

Of course, the problem with regulating out-of-hours email is that it's very hard to stop people from picking up their messages, even if they know they technically have the right to ignore them. We've all now been conditioned to jump every time we feel a vibration in one of our pocketed regions, and while it's one thing to know you don't *have* to check your email, it's another to shrug off that nagging feeling that you *just might be missing something super-important* as you watch message after message stack up.

INAPPROPRIATE PLACES I HAVE CHECKED MY WORK EMAIL

On holiday

At the family dinner table

Out with friends

On a first date

On a last date

Up a mountain

On the beach

In a Buddhist temple

On a 'reconnecting with nature' camping trip

In bed

In the bath

On the loo

After a few too many drinks

After many too many drinks

The onus is therefore on the sender to respect their recipient's time. Stick to work hours wherever possible and avoid weekends and holidays. Be mindful that your recipient's work hours may be different to yours; try to accommodate schedule or time zone differences as much as is reasonable. For bonus points, avoid emailing on Monday mornings and Friday afternoons, when no one will appreciate the disturbance.

Ah, you might say, *but they don't have to answer them straight away! I, the super-conscientious employee, just want to complete my to-do list and send all of my emails as soon as possible. I don't mind putting in the extra time! In fact, I like answering emails in my pyjamas! And that way, I'm not keeping anyone waiting on my response – I'm doing them a favour!*

No, you're not, and your colleagues hate you.

This goes back to the paradox of email: here, you are enjoying the convenience of email while forcing the stress of it onto your recipient. Even if you're not requiring or even expecting anyone to respond to your messages immediately, they will likely feel pressure to do so. By emailing at that time yourself, you have set an unreasonable norm – and in doing so you are exhibiting poor etiquette.

Still really want to write emails at an unsociable hour? Learn how to use your email service's scheduling feature.

How quickly must you respond to an email?

If you were to ask anyone what constitutes good email etiquette, they would probably say something to the effect of 'responding promptly'. But what exactly counts as 'prompt'?

This is one of the main sources of email stress. Because there are no real established norms around how swiftly you should reply, we all feel obliged to do so as soon as possible – even though the whole point of email is that it's asynchronous.

If you're following Inbox Zero, you should be able to turn around simple emails without much delay, and at least within a day. The problem comes when you need to provide a longer response or complete some kind of task before replying.

While there's no one-stop answer as to how long you can leave people waiting, there is an easy workaround: ask them. People have a misguided assumption that etiquette must be unspoken, but transparency is often the best way to ward off potential misunderstandings. If you're not sure when your full response is needed, reply first to confirm a deadline and make sure you're on the same page. All you need to say is something like, 'Is it OK if I get this to you tomorrow?' or 'I plan to have this with you by Monday,' or 'I need to think about this – when do you need my answer?'

It's also true that fast replies are not always the best etiquette. There can be considerable advantages to delaying a response, particularly if you're on an email thread with multiple people. Here, it's often better to hold back a while and see how things play out. It may be that your input is not even needed in the end – and you can rest safe in the knowledge that you just decreased the world's email traffic by one more message.

When to send an email, part 2

Before you put fingertips to keyboard, stop and think: is email really the right medium for this message? In most workplaces, email has become the default means of getting anything done, but it shouldn't be. Indeed, the same qualities that make email perfect for some tasks make it terrible for others.

Email is good for non-urgent communications and simple back-and-forths. It's good for sharing documents, starting a paper trail and distributing information to lots of people at once.

Here's what it's *not* good for:

- **Immediate responses.** A key selling point of email is its *asynchrony*; you can send an email at one time and your recipient can pick it up whenever is convenient to them. This means that you can't assume you'll get an immediate answer. Sometimes it's better to text, instant message, shout across the room or (gasp) pick up the phone.

- **Nuance.** It's hard to express tone over email. Efficiency can easily be misinterpreted as aloofness and politeness can come across as standoffish. Anything that requires a bit of tact or delicacy is best suited to a medium where you can use verbal and non-verbal cues (i.e. old-fashioned talking) to make sure your meaning gets across.

- **Discussion and debate.** Email is not a discursive medium. Long email threads between multiple parties can quickly get confusing, with everyone weighing in and no one sure what their role in the discussion is meant to be. If you need to have a group debate or come to a joint decision, schedule a meeting – and email a memo round afterwards.

- **Confidences.** There's no deleting an email once it's sent, and after that it's completely out of your control. An email can be forwarded to anyone without you knowing, so stick to in-person meetings if it's a sensitive subject. Keep in mind that your work email is not private: your company likely has access to it, and there's always the chance you could be hacked. Keep it professional.

SHOULD YOU SEND AN EMAIL?

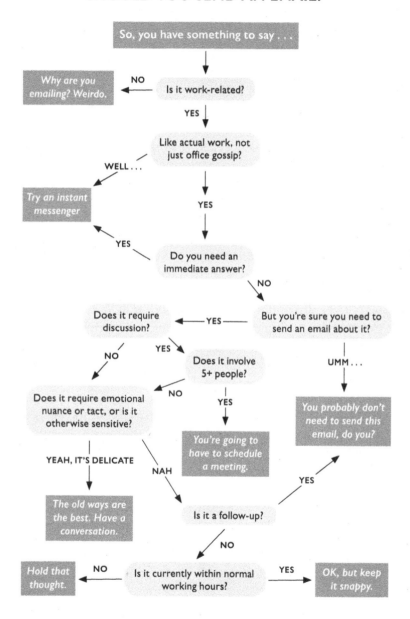

EMAIL ALTERNATIVES

The phone call

What's worse than a work email? A work phone call.

That's not strictly true. In the correct circumstances, a phone call can be the best way to get something done. It's faster than email and benefits from tone of voice, making it much better suited to back-and-forth discussions and more sensitive situations. You can ask a question and they answer – no need for a 12-part email chain and frantic analyses of whether the fact they only sent a one-line response means they hate you or they're just a bit busy.

No, the problem is *unscheduled* phone calls. You're settling down at your computer, you're just getting in the zone – and your desk phone starts ringing with an unrecognised number. The horror. The solution is simple: if you want to call someone, set a time first. There's nothing worse than scrambling to pick up the receiver before the ringing disturbs your coworkers, only to find it's someone you don't want to speak to, wanting to have a conversation you're not ready to have. Advance notice means you can both carve out time in your diaries and make sure you're prepared. (The exception is if it's genuinely urgent and you only need a really quick answer – phone calls under a minute get a free pass.)

If someone calls out of the blue asking to speak to a colleague, there is only ever one correct response, even if they're sat right next to you:

'Oh I'm sorry, they're in a meeting – shall I let them know you called?'

Voicemails

While the phone call has its merits, the voicemail has none. It's entirely redundant. It's calling to say you called. On top of that, it's useless as a means of conveying any actual information. It takes about 60 times longer to check than an email, and you always get to that part halfway through where someone starts reciting their phone number, you scramble for a pen, fumble to note it down – *wait, was that 6-2-3 or 6-3-2?* – and have to start the whole recording from the top. It's a waste of everyone's time.

If you can't get through to someone on the phone and want to leave a message, there are many more effective ways. Write an email. Send a text. Scribble a Post-it Note. Write a message, stick it into a bottle and drop it down the nearest drain.

THINGS I'D RATHER DO THAN CHECK MY VOICEMAIL

Answer all my emails

File my expenses

Share an 'interesting fact' about myself at the start of a meeting

Write in Comic Sans for a week

Fix the office printer

Staple my finger

Clean the coffee machine

Volunteer for the work fun run

Offer to organise the Christmas party

Pay someone else to check my voicemail

Conference calls

If you don't like phone calls, try doing it with six people on the line.

Every conference call starts roughly the same way. First you have at least five minutes of saying hello, which tends to go something like this:

You have entered the conference call.

'Hi! Is that John?'

'No, it's Janet.'

'Hi Janet! This is Nell.'

'Hi Nell!'

'Hi Janet! This is Bob.'

'Hi Bob!'

'So are we just waiting on John?'

'Yes, we're just waiting for John.'

'Does he have the login?'

'I'll send him a note.'

'. . .'

'Maybe we should get started and he can join later. Janet, do you want to begin?'

'Sure, let me just start by saying –'

'Hi, this is John.'

'Hi John! This is Nell.'

'Hi Nell!'

'Hi John! This is Bob.'

'Hi Bob!'

'Hi John! This is Janet.'

'Hi Janet!'

'Janet was just about to get started . . .'

Once everyone has joined, you are allowed exactly one comment about the weather, after which all small talk is banned. Try not to talk over each other; remember that people dialing in internationally may have a slight delay in response. Stick to the time allotted for the call, and remember to leave a few minutes for the extended goodbyes:

'OK great, thank you!'

'No, thank you.'

'Thanks everyone.'

'OK, thanks, bye.'

'Bye.'

'Yes, bye.'

'And thanks.'

'Thank you.'

'Bye.'

'Speak soon.'

'Looking forward to it.'

'Bye.'

(*Repeat ad infinitum until someone finally builds up the courage to put down the receiver first.*)

To avoid the above, conference calls should be used sparingly and kept to the minimum number of people possible.

HOW TO WRITE AN EMAIL (YES, REALLY)

S O, YOU'RE READY to write an email. You've thought about it, you're sure that email is the best medium, and you're ready to compose.

First of all, let's recap that golden rule of email etiquette: everything you do should be in service of reducing the burden of email on your recipient. Concision and clarity are your guiding principles.

In this respect, emails diverge significantly from traditional letter-writing protocol. When writing a letter, you would usually expect to open with some small talk, ask after your correspondent's health, thank them for their previous letter, and so on; launching straight into whatever you want from that person would be considered rather abrupt.

Email turns this on its head. It's perfectly fine – indeed preferable – to get straight to it. Far from being impolite, brevity in email shows a respect for your reader's time. Merlin Mann has some solid advice on this: 'Assume that everyone you're communicating with is smarter than you and cares more than you and is busier than you.'

If you're emailing in a business context, you are probably doing so out of necessity, not nicety; you don't need to try to disguise that fact with generic pleasantries, which will likely only come off as inauthentic anyway. Unless you have a genuine reason to be concerned about your recipient's wellbeing, there is no need to start your message with 'How are you?'

Making your email as easy as possible for your recipient to deal with means being crystal clear about what you're asking and, crucially, what action you expect the other person to take. If you need a 'yes' or 'no' answer, make sure there's a 'yes' or 'no' question. Include all the necessary information in your first email, so that you don't end up drawing it out into a string of back-and-forth messages. If you need to set up a meeting, don't just say you need to set up a meeting; suggest a specific time and place.

Then, wrap it up. Web designer Mike Davidson holds that no email needs to be longer than five sentences long. In 2007, he set up the website five.sentenc.es, which encourages people to adopt a five-sentence limit and copy a link to the website in their email signature to explain the brevity to recipients (there's also a four.sentenc.es, three.sentenc.es and even two.sentenc.es for those who like a challenge). If it sounds a bit restrictive, give it a try. You'll likely find that you can respond to most things in that space. If you have to scroll your screen to get to the end of a message, it's probably too long.

Subject lines

A subject line could be the difference between someone reading your email and ignoring it, so put a bit of thought into it. Keep it short and obvious: your reader should be able to tell from the subject line what they can expect from the rest of the email. Remember it will likely be read on mobile, so you can probably fit a maximum of around six words before it gets cut off.

Never leave the subject line blank; that's just rude. Don't put the whole message in the subject line and leave the email blank; that's a text message. And unless you're sending out a mass-marketing email (which: don't), don't try to be funny and definitely don't try to fool people into opening your email with clickbait headlines or sneaky ruses. The worst trick I've seen is a marketer starting the subject 'Re:' to make it look as if they were responding to an email I'd already sent. Do not do this. Yes, your recipient may be duped into opening the email, but you can bet they will angry-delete it in less time than it took you to type those two letters.

If the email is urgent, you may note that in the subject – but exercise restraint. Each time you play the 'urgent' card, you're decreasing its value. You can also use electronic labels to flag an email's level of importance, but it's best to avoid this unless absolutely critical. If something were unimportant, you presumably wouldn't be sending an email about it in the first place (and if you would, go back and start this chapter again, as you clearly haven't been paying attention.)

How to begin

You don't need to use a greeting every time you send an email. Greet your recipient in the first email, but if it turns into a back-and-forth thread, treat it like a conversation – you don't have to keep interjecting with 'hello' every time it's your turn to speak.

How you greet someone depends on how well you know them and the level of formality required for the situation. A lawyer is probably going to have a different standard protocol to a nightclub owner. Honestly, 'Hi' is usually fine. In particularly formal contexts, err on the side of formality and use 'Dear' the first time, then take the age-old etiquette shortcut and simply follow the other person's lead. For close colleagues, you can keep things informal.

Always use someone's name if you can, and for goodness' sake make sure you spell it correctly. I go by Victoria or Vicki, but I've regularly been Viktoria, Vicky, Vikki, Vickey and Victor (and once, for some reason, Hazel). It's usually fine to address people on a first-name basis, but go for their title and surname in more official business dealings, or if you want to show a higher degree of respect for their position. It's a good idea to use someone's full title first time round if it's anything other than Mr/Mrs/Ms/Miss, as in Lord, Lady, Sir, Dame, Dr, Professor and so on – some people can be quite particular about that.

'To whom it may concern' or 'Dear Sir or Madam' (or worse, 'Dear Sirs') only make it look as if you haven't done your homework, or have copy-pasted the same email to a bunch of different people. Why should someone bother reading your email if you don't even know who you're writing it to? The same goes for referring to someone by their job title. If you really can't find out the person's name, you're probably best just sticking to 'Hi'.

How do you address an email to the Queen?

You don't. You send a snail-mail letter to her private secretary.

Striking the right tone

It's notoriously difficult to convey tone in email. You don't have the benefit of non-verbal cues such as facial expression, tone of voice or body language, so you need to use your words to make your intentions as clear as possible.

A common mistake is to try to be *too* polite, which can end up back-firing and appearing haughty and aloof. Consider the following example:

'Please could you get back to me by Friday?'

It's perfectly respectful, clear, and gets the point across with minimal fuss. Now, consider the same sentiment wrapped up in more formal language:

'I would be much obliged if you could kindly respond to this message at your earliest convenience.'

This is unhelpful, unspecific and makes you sound like a pompous arse.

USEFUL TRANSLATIONS OF COMMON EMAIL PHRASES

'Apologies for the delayed response.' – *It's just the law that you have to write this at the start of every email.*

'Hope you're well.' – *Small talk over, now let me list my demands.*

'Just following up/checking in/touching base/circling back.' – *Oi, why haven't you replied to this yet?*

'Not sure if you saw my last message. . .' – *You definitely saw my last message.*

'Did I miss your response?' – *We both know I didn't.*

'Sorry to chase. . .' – *Sorry not sorry.*

'As per my previous email. . .' – *Keep up, slowpoke.*

'To be clear. . .' – *How are you still not getting this?*

'Does that make sense?' – *Are you stupid?*

'Let me know if you have any questions.' – *Don't.*

'Thanks in advance.' – *Just so we're clear, you have absolutely no choice about whether to do this or not.*

'It'd be great to hear back from you asap.' – *Like, yesterday.*

In praise of concision, or how to email like a CEO

There's concise, and then there's *concise*. In 2017, Buzzfeed writer Katie Notopoulos decided to try what she calls 'emailing like a CEO' – answering every message almost instantly, but with a very short response.[4]

Notopoulos says that she first picked up on this trend when emailing CEOs in her role as a tech and business reporter. Mark Cuban, owner of the Dallas Mavericks basketball team and one of the investors on US TV series *Shark Tank*, has a reputation for emailing quick, one-word responses, and she noticed that her editor-in-chief took a similar approach in his emails to her. So, she decided to give it a go. 'I thought it'd be a fun stunt to write about, but I also thought it might be helpful for myself,' she says.

The key to emailing like a CEO is to respond as quickly as possible and get straight to the point, with absolutely zero preamble. It could be just one or two words. 'Thanks.' 'OK.' 'What's the latest?' Grammar is optional. Amazon's Jeff Bezos takes things even further, reportedly making a habit of forwarding customer emails to his employees with a single character: '?'

Notopoulos did this for a week, and found that it made a big difference. 'It was great,' she says. 'I didn't realise how much email hung over my head like a little dark storm cloud all day long.' She says she felt more productive and less stressed, and not just when it came to email: 'I felt so productive dealing with my inbox that I also felt like I was more productive in the other work that I was doing.'

Notopoulos has kept up the habit as much as possible. Where she used to read emails on her phone, then wait until she was at a computer to answer them, she now treats them more like tweets, prioritising a rapid response over a perfectly composed one. 'It's much better to actually get it done than it is to have it worded perfectly,' she says. She sometimes just uses the suggested replies on Gmail – those chipper automated responses based on an AI analysis of an email's content.

A note of caution, however: emailing like a boss might make you feel more zen, but it's not always appropriate. There's a thin line between a short response and a terse response. Someone you work with every day is probably fine with you responding in a word or two, but less well-known senders merit a few more niceties. Just because you're being concise doesn't mean you can neglect your pleases and thank-yous.

Notopoulos admits that emailing like a CEO won't work for everyone. People with jobs in sales or customer service, for example, may have to sacrifice some efficiency for a higher level of courtesy. There's also a power dynamic at play here: perhaps this is 'emailing like a CEO' because only the CEO can get away with it. As Notopoulos says: 'Being the boss or being the CEO affords you the ability to be slightly rude to your underlings over email.'

Corporate jargon

Another aspect of email that sometimes needs to be decoded – and, frankly, that should be avoided as much as possible – is corporate jargon. The corporate jargoneer is in many ways the opposite of the 'CEO emailer'. Rather than keeping things brief, he (and it's usually a he) sees each email as an official missive to be carefully crafted using as many fancy-sounding professional phrases as possible, so that you end up with a lot of words that say nothing at all. He writes as if his whole vocabulary comes from the 'business books' section on Amazon. He uses words like 'synergy' and 'blue-sky think-ing' unironically. He sporadically capitalises words that aren't proper nouns. He uses 'action' as a transitive verb.

Some corporate jargoneers don't even limit themselves to email. One of the worst I've come across was at a dinner party, when I asked a fellow guest what he did for a living and he described himself as an 'architect'. What did he design? 'Solutions.' After a bit of careful probing, I found out that he was, in fact, a management consultant.

Avoid corporate buzzwords and clichés at all costs. They are the antithesis of concision and clarity, and make you look like you're trying way too hard.

Corporate jargon bingo

Received an email from a corporate jargon waffler? See if you can get a full house!

thesaurus abuse	an acronym you don't recognise	noun used as a verb	'synergy'
'think outside the box'	portmanteau they just thought up	things aren't bad, they're 'sub-optimal'	'innovate'
more than one $20 word	calls people 'assets'	'110%'	randomly capitalised word
shoehorns in company slogan	appoints self spokesperson for a larger group	'disrupt'	overly formal sign-off
insincere thanks	mixed metaphor	Steve Jobs reference	male author

Sorry, just one more thing

A final point on email language: don't pepper your messages with pointless qualifiers. There's a common tendency, particularly among women, to try to 'soften' emails with words like 'just' or 'sorry' or 'actually' or 'I think' (or 'Sorry, I just think that actually . . .'). But while you may think you're being polite, this can have the effect of undermining your message.

In 2015, tech worker Tami Reiss built a plugin for Gmail called Just Not Sorry, which automatically highlights these qualifiers, like a spell-checker for self-doubt. She explains that she originally came up with the idea after having brunch with some other female businesswomen. They watched an Amy Schumer skit in which the comedian plays a scientist who struggles to talk about her work through constant unnecessary apologies. 'I said, "I want help when it comes to stopping saying sorry,"' recalls Reiss, who now works as a product lead at business platform Justworks. 'I want to stop saying sorry.'

Women have been socially conditioned to act submissive and meek, to be stereotypically ladylike and to reflect this in our speech. We've been taught to apologise for everything – sorry for interrupting, sorry that you spilled your coffee on me, sorry for taking up space, sorry just in case. We're apologising for existing.

Not only is this unnecessary, but it can make you look less capable and confident, not to mention that it diminishes the power of the word 'sorry' when you actually mean it. It also sets you up on the wrong side of a power imbalance, immediately positioning you as the weaker party. 'If I show up late to a meeting and I say, "Oh, I'm so sorry I'm late," the power dynamic immediately sends a signal that you are more important than I am,' Reiss says. 'If I show up and I say, "Thanks so much for waiting for me" the power dynamic is completely inverted – *you* waited for *me*.'

Say sorry when you need to, but don't temper your message to massage other people's egos. Good etiquette does not mean being a pushover, and you can be confident and direct without being rude.

Signing off

There is no good way to sign off an email, so just go for 'Best wishes' or 'Best'. Yes it's bland, yes it's boring, but it is inoffensive, balances being formal enough without being pretentious, and is therefore the best option out of a decidedly bad bunch.

'Thanks' isn't terrible, but can be a bit presumptive. 'Thanks in advance' is just rude (you might as well write, 'Try getting out of that one now'). 'Kind regards' or 'Best regards' is unnecessarily staid for most emails. You could use 'Yours faithfully' or 'Yours sincerely' if you're writing an email like an official letter, but this is only really necessary for particularly formal occasions, such as a cover letter for a job application. 'Cheers', 'Ciao', 'Ta' and so on are fine for close colleagues but not for people you don't know well.

Follow-ups

The three ugliest words in the English language are 'just following up'. (The three most beautiful, if you're wondering: 'unsubscribe from list'.)

These annoying little chasers always claim to be 'just' following up or touching base or checking in or circling back, or whatever, as if it's no big deal – 'just' following up! In fact, of course, they're clearly designed to purposefully ramp up the

WHAT YOUR DEFAULT EMAIL SIGN-OFF SAYS ABOUT YOU

Best wishes – *You are normal. You don't rock the boat. You are utterly unremarkable (which, in a business context, is entirely appropriate).*

Best – *You are also normal, if a little more time-pressed.*

BW – *You've taken a perfectly acceptable sign-off and turned it into an abomination. Do you still use text speak in your text messages too?*

All the best/All my best – *You've actively thought about your email sign-off. You really want to do something different, but you can't quite bring yourself to stray too far from the norm.*

Kind regards – *You're a bit socially awkward. Your idea of dress-down Friday is slightly loosening your tie.*

Yours faithfully/Yours sincerely – *You're desperate to sound sophisticated, but you just come across as a bit of a tool.*

Cheers – *You're the joker of the office. You tell people that you don't have colleagues, you have 'friends that you work with'.*

Ta – *You're northern.*

Love from – *You're either under ten years old or an HR incident waiting to happen.*

Greetings – *You are an alien. You come in peace.*

pressure and make you feel guilty for not already responding.

Avoid sending follow-ups. Frankly, they're unflattering, making you look at best demanding and at worst desperate. If you need to give someone a nudge, then get straight to the point and be clear about what you're after. As Tami Reiss puts it: 'You're not *just* checking in, you're checking in for a reason. If you're *just* checking in? You're not my mother.'

If you absolutely have to chase a response, you get one shot at it. *One.* By sending a follow-up, you've just *doubled* your imposition on someone else's inbox. If you still don't get a response, it's time to face the facts: they're just not interested.

THE FINER DETAILS

How to use CC

Oh, how much easier life would be if we could all agree on how to use CC.

Here's the deal:

- The 'to' field is for the primary recipients of the email, who are expected to respond.
- The 'CC' field is for people who need to see the email for reference only and don't need to respond.

So many people seem unable to grasp this, but it makes email so much easier. If you're in the 'to' field, you should respond; if you're on CC, don't. The most recent edition of the famous Debrett's etiquette handbook dedicates just two pages to the topic of digital communication (about the same as it has on how to address a bishop), yet even it makes room for this crucial distinction. Repeat it after me, write it in your diary, tattoo it on your arm: *this is how to use CC.*

When is it necessary to include people on CC? In aid of eliminating email excess, you should limit the number of recipients on an email to as few as possible, but there are some situations in which a CC is a necessary courtesy. If you're referring directly to someone in an email, it's polite to copy them in; no one likes to feel others are talking about them behind their back. If you're sending an email about a group project, CC the other members of the team so no one feels left out. Aside from these situations, be judicious. CCs can be like party invitations if you're not careful – send one to one person and suddenly you feel obliged to add everyone else in the same group. Before you know it, the guest list is over capacity, the bar has run dry, and no one can remember the reason they're gathered there in the first place.

And while CC can be a nice email courtesy, it can also go the other way. If you're mid-email-chain with one person and suddenly throw in a third party on CC, you risk breaking the rapport. Be particularly mindful if the conversation is at all personal in nature; remember that anyone you loop in will be able to read past messages in the email thread.

In some cases, abuse of the CC field can be downright rude. Ever received an email asking you to do something, or complaining about how you've handled something, where the sender has oh-so-thoughtfully decided to copy in your boss? This is what I believe in Etiquette-land they call 'a dick move'.

Copying in someone's supervisor undermines them, as it basically says that you don't trust them to deal with the issue themselves. It can even come across as a kind of blackmail – 'Don't respond how I want you to and you'll be in trouble!' I once worked with a man who insisted on CCing my male colleague into every email he sent me, even though he had been informed multiple times it was my responsibility to deal with him (more's the pity). Don't be that asshole.

When, if at all, to BCC

Using BCC, CC's sneaky sibling, is playing with etiquette fire. The 'B' in BCC stands for 'blind', and it means that the primary recipient of your email will not see that you have copied someone else into the correspondence. They are a silent witness.

Sneakiness is generally poor etiquette, and you should avoid using BCC most of the time. If you really need to loop someone into an email confidentially, for example to establish a paper trail, Debrett's has you covered: instead of blind-copying, 'the email should be forwarded on to the third party, with a short note explaining any confidentiality, after its distribution'.[5]

That said, as with CC, there are a few circumstances in which BCC is not only acceptable but admirable:

- When you're emailing a group of people and don't want to reveal their identities and/or email addresses to everyone else in the group. In these situations, you should send the email to yourself and BCC everyone else. This is good etiquette, as you generally shouldn't hand out someone else's email address without permission. There are also cases where attaching someone's name to a group email may be sensitive, compromising or even illegal. In 2016, a London NHS trust was fined for revealing the names of 730 people who used an HIV service, after a staff member accidentally put all the recipients in the 'to' field instead of BCC. Yikes.

- When you're sending a mass email and want to avoid a reply-allpocalypse (see below). The advantage here is that someone on BCC cannot reply to other people on BCC, so you prevent a mass discussion from breaking out among respondents.

- When you're employing BCC in the service of saving another person's inbox. This is a truly noble etiquette manoeuvre whereby you remove someone from an email chain without just cutting them off cold. Here's how it works: let's say someone includes your colleague on an email, but you know they don't need to be part of the discussion. Instead of replying all, you can reply to the sender and move your colleague to the BCC field. This means that they will see your response – and know that you have things under control – but won't be disturbed by any further messages. When you do this, state in the email copy that you're moving them to BCC, so everyone's on the same page. For example: 'Hi Sophie, I'll deal with this – moving Caroline to BCC to save her inbox.' It's the ultimate act of email etiquette self-sacrifice.

Replies vs reply-all

When to reply or reply-all is an important judgement call. On the one hand, you don't want to needlessly hit reply-all and bring more unnecessary email into the world. On the other, you don't want to look underhand, or like you're talking about people behind their backs.

If reply-all is the norm on a particular email thread, then you should follow suit (but remember the rules of CC – no need to reply at all if you're only on CC). If you are sending an email to lots of people seeking individual input, do your bit to establish good reply hygiene by explicitly stating in the email that responses should be sent off-thread. It's likely many will ignore this, but if enough of us keep fighting the good fight, we might eventually make some headway.

How to avoid a reply-allpocalypse

When reply-all goes wrong, it goes really wrong. A reply-allpocalypse usually occurs when someone accidentally addresses an email to a company distribution list, thus sending it to far more people than they intended. Many workplaces use lists like these to make it easy to email whole departments, or even the entire company, at once; you only have to type one email address to reach potentially thousands of people.

You know how it begins: someone accidentally sends an email to the wrong list. They meant to send it just to their team, but their finger slipped and they've sent it to the entire office. Oh, and all the global offices, too. It starts off innocently enough. Rather than just ignoring the email, someone decides to respond – not realising that their reply will also get disseminated to the all-office mailing list.

> *Sorry, I think you've sent this to the wrong email. I don't think it's meant for me.*

Everyone now receives this message too. Another comes in.

> *Hi, this isn't meant for me. Please can you take me off this thread.*

Next, the automatic out-of-office responses start to ping back. The scale of the incident begins to make itself known.

> *I don't think I'm supposed to be on this either! :)*

Hi, I don't even know who any of you are, I'm on here by mistake. Can you take me off this email?

Put the kettle on and make yourself comfortable, because the reply-all demon has now been summoned, and it will be holding your and everyone else's inbox hostage for the foreseeable. As each reply comes in, more people see the original all-office email, and then the replies too. The penny starts to drop. Some bright spark will cling to the delusion that it's still possible to get the situation under control.

Please can everyone just stop asking people to take them off this thread, as this only results in more emails.

Replies about not replying start to proliferate.

Everyone, just stop replying to this thread.

Lol you realise your reply is also a reply :)

The thread gains steam. Someone remembers you can send gifs by email. Memes begin to spread. The office is buzzing; the reply-all storm is now the only thing anyone can talk about in real life, too.

The pleas get increasingly angry. The all-caps come out. There are way too many exclamation marks for a professional context.

OH MY GOD, PLEASE TAKE ME OFF THIS THREAD!!!!!

There's always someone who sees an opportunity in adversity:

Well while we're all here (lol!) here's a reminder about the charity fun run this weekend! It's not too late to sign up!

By this point, the original sender has disappeared into a manager's office somewhere with their head hung low. A terse official note makes the rounds.

Dear colleagues,

This email has been sent in error. Please DO NOT RESPOND to this email or any before it. IT are working on closing the thread down.

Could all staff please remember that the all-office email address is not to be used unless explicitly approved by a manager, as detailed in our email policy guidelines, attached here for your reference.

A few last replies filter through, and then the demon retreats. Until next time.

What should you do when you find yourself caught up in a reply-allpocalypse? A definitive answer can be found in a 2016 issue of the *New York Times*, which featured a story by reporter Daniel Victor with the headline, 'When I'm Mistakenly Put on an Email Chain, Should I Hit "Reply All" Asking to Be Removed?' The body of the article, reproduced here in full, read:

No.

Beneath that was a reporting credit: 'The *New York Times*'s internal email system contributed to this report.'

If you find yourself a victim of a reply-allpocalypse, don't reply. If you want to maintain your sanity, you can also set up an email rule to block the distribution list address, so that you don't receive any further replies to it – at least until the storm has passed.

Meanwhile, just be glad you don't work for a larger organisation. In 2016, a reply-allpocalypse hit the NHS (which apparently has some work to do on its email skills) when an administrator tried to set up a new distribution list for their unit, but ended up accidentally including every NHSmail account in England – all 840,000 of them. In a report following the incident, the NHS wrote that, 'On an average day NHSmail handles between three and five million emails; but between 08:29 and 09:45 on 14 November the service received $c.500$ million which needed to be processed.'

THE THREE CIRCUMSTANCES UNDER WHICH IT IS APPROPRIATE TO SEND AN ALL-OFFICE EMAIL

1. When there's a genuine emergency ('There's a fire')

2. To convey a company-wide announcement ('You're all fired')

3. Free food

Out-of-office replies

As you probably know, if you're going to be away from your work email for a while, it's a good idea to set up an out-of-office, or automatic reply. That way, when someone tries to email you, they'll get an automated response explaining that you're not at work, won't be replying to email and frankly couldn't give a hoot about their message.

The point of the out-of-office (OOO) is twofold. Firstly, it lets people know not to expect an answer to their questions, so they aren't left hanging in digital limbo awaiting your response. Secondly, it absolves you of unread email guilt, as your inbox is left safe in the hands of an attentive robot. Ironically, it's probably the only time that everyone who emails you will receive a timely response, albeit not a very useful one.

Your out-of-office message should contain a few crucial details – most importantly, the date you'll be back. You may also wish to include the contact details for a colleague who is handling your work in your absence, but make sure you get their permission first.

Keep your message to the point. Corporate jargon has crept insidiously into the out-of-office response, so that suddenly everyone is informing you not that they're on holiday, but that they're on 'annual leave' – as if they're embarking on some sort of transformative life experience and not just flopping on a beach in Mallorca for a week. Don't go too far the other way, though – no one wants to get an auto-response gloating about how you're *probably busy sipping pina coladas in the sun!* while they're scrambling to sort out whatever mess you left at the office.

Digital calendars

Digital calendars are a mainstay of office software suites, and can be very helpful to schedule and keep track of meetings and other events. But there are a few points of etiquette to remember. Please note that a calendar invite does not constitute an actual invitation. You need to include a message explaining to your recipient what the occasion is, and actually inviting them to it. Just inserting yourself into someone's digital space by plonking an appointment in their diary is incredibly presumptuous.

Confirm the time and location of the meeting before you send a calendar invite; you shouldn't change these after the fact unless it's completely unavoidable. And please, don't even think about using one of those infuriating scheduling apps that forces everyone to list every possible moment they potentially might be free over the next two weeks in order to find a mutually agreeable time to meet. If you're organising an event, it's on you to actually organise the event.

A LIFE BEYOND EMAIL? THE ETIQUETTE
OF INSTANT MESSAGING

COULD IT BE that there is an alternative to the horror show of email? In the past decade, instant messaging tools such as Slack have entered the workplace to try to pick up some of the slack (sorry) from our overflowing inboxes. Slack, and tools like it, are different from email in that they are intended solely for internal communications and put a focus on real-time messaging – think WhatsApp, but for work.

Slack is the Marmite of office tools. Some people love it, others loathe it, but whichever side of the debate you look at, I've never known people exhibit so much passionate feeling about a piece of enterprise software. For the lovers, Slack reduces inbox bloat, streamlines communication, and plays the role of a digital water-cooler to boot. For the loathers, it's just email on steroids.

A couple of simple rules can mean the difference between your instant messenger being a time-saver or a time-suck. First, recognise what instant messaging is good for. Unlike email, it is ideal for quick answers and back-and-forth chat. It is not appropriate for information dumps or drawn-out discussions. Treat it like text messaging. Messages should be short, informal and relatively disposable.

Second, make sure you've set it up in a way that is conducive to productivity. Instant messengers let you send private messages to people, but a key selling point is group chats, or channels. The key to an effective channel is to be clear about what it is for and keep it limited to people who need to be in that group – like when you CC people on email.

But don't get too excited; we're not about to see the death of email any time soon. While I know plenty of offices that have started using instant messaging tools in the past few years, I haven't heard of a single one that has stopped using email. As Slack co-founder and CTO Cal Henderson said onstage at a 2018 *Wired* event: 'Email is the cockroach of the internet.' It's not going anywhere.

All the annoying people you'll find on Slack

The backchanneller

The backchanneller has at least six chats open at any one time. While everyone is discussing something in the group channel, they're sending you private messages to suss out your thoughts on the sly. You're initially flattered that they value your views – until you realise they're doing the same to everyone else too.

The meme fiend

Usually one of the younger team members, the meme fiend rarely responds in words, instead finding an animated gif for every occasion. You have to admit that it's impressive how they manage to find a suitable image so quickly. Whether it's always work-appropriate is another question.

The @all abuser

Most instant messengers have an option to push a notification out to all members of a channel, such as by tagging @all. It's the Slack equivalent to reply-all and should thus be used very sparingly – but there's always one person who gets a bit trigger-happy. 'Hey @all anyone want a cup of tea?' '@all anyone seen my mug?' 'Thanks @all I found it.'

The over-organiser

This is the kind of person who colour-codes their meeting notes and indexes their stationery drawer. On Slack, their organisational obsession expresses itself in creating channels for every possible group permutation, inventing a new one for each individual project so that every time you go to post you end up spending more time thinking about which channel you're supposed to be writing in than what you're actually going to say.

The late adopter

There's always one office curmudgeon who drags their feet when it comes to new technologies. The late adopter is *technically* on the system, having begrudgingly signed up after a pointed email from the boss's office, but when it comes to actually getting a response, you'd be more likely to get through to them by carrier pigeon.

LinkedIn

One last thing on the subject of workplace communications: *please* stop inviting me to join your professional network on LinkedIn.

Most social media is best kept well away from office politics, but LinkedIn is the exception, focused as it is on professional connections rather than people you actually like. For many, the site is little more than an online CV dump; you make a profile when looking for your first job and return only when you need to update your experience (or, if you've failed to adequately filter your email preferences, then every single day when you receive an email breathlessly informing you that someone has viewed your profile, or that you appeared in 41 searches this week, or that you really ought to congratulate someone on their 'work anniversary', as if that's a thing).

Aside from the occasional self-promotional update, most of us feel little urge to actually post on LinkedIn. For a special few, however, LinkedIn is not just a useful resource to occasionally check someone's job title; it's a way of life.

You know the ones: they usually describe themselves as an 'entrepreneur', 'innovator' or 'thought leader', but it's never clear exactly how they make a living (bonus points if they use the term 'digital nomad'). They collect LinkedIn endorsements with the keenness of a primary-schooler earning gold stars, and write prolific posts doling out business advice no one asked for, always with a liberal smattering of motivational hashtags.

They also often do that thing.

You know, that thing.

That thing where they type their post in simple sentences.

And separate each one.

With a line break between them.

Maybe because they think it makes them look important.

Maybe because they read that's what Thought Leaders ought to do.

Or maybe just so that you're forced . . .

. . . to click the 'see more' button.

When it comes to connecting with others over LinkedIn, people take one of two approaches: they either only connect with people they actually know, or they connect with anyone and everyone, racking up as many strangers as they can in their imaginary business network. Let's get this clear: the first way is correct, the second is not.

But don't just take my word for it. Ask Kat Boogaard, a freelance writer on the business beat who once wrote a piece for careers site The Muse in which she extolled the virtues of accepting every LinkedIn request. *It broadens your horizons!* she argued. *It opens you to new opportunities! It gets your foot in the door!* As long as people sent a personal note with their invitation, she wrote, she was willing to connect.[6]

A few months later, she realised her mistake and wrote a rebuttal to her own article.[7] The problem was that, after she published the piece, everyone who read it tried to connect with

THE BEST WAYS TO REACH ME AT WORK, RANKED BY AVERAGE SPEED OF RESPONSE

1. *Shouting across the office*

2. *Slack message*

3. *Phone call*

4. *Email*

5. *A meeting*

6. *Snail mail*

7. *Morse code*

8. *Omens in my coffee grinds*

9. *LinkedIn*

10. *Voicemail*

her – and she couldn't turn them away for fear of looking like a hypocrite. 'Before I knew it, I had hundreds of requests from people I'd never met,' she recalls.

Her LinkedIn became largely useless. She had a large network, but it was meaningless; most of the people she added weren't even in her industry. Boogaard says that it put her off posting updates about her career or accomplishments – it seemed too weird to share that with strangers.

Keep your connections to people you know, or at the very least people who may have a shared professional interest. Many people don't regularly check LinkedIn, so if you want to send a message, you're much better trying to find their email than sending them an 'InMail'.

Oh, and guys: don't try to proposition people through LinkedIn. No, you don't look suave in that suit. No, we're not impressed by your job title. This is literally the least sexy place on the internet, and you are a creep.

SLIDING INTO YOUR DMs

THE ART OF ROMANCE

———————

FIVE GOLDEN RULES:

1. Consent, consent, consent

2. Be bold and make the first move

3. Don't play games

4. Casper, don't ghost

5. No creeps allowed

Digital technologies have changed the way we meet, flirt and fall in love. Pre-internet, your dating pool was limited to people you actually knew in real life, or could be introduced to by friends or family. If you were really desperate, you might put a personal ad in a newspaper or lonely hearts column (the original Craigslist).

Online dating opened the floodgates, giving us all access to a much broader range of potential partners. These days, around 20 per cent of people meet their partners online – a number that increases to around 70 per cent among same-sex couples.[1] Some research even suggests that online dating has contributed to an increase in interracial marriages, by making it easier for people to date outside of traditional social circles.[2]

The idea of digitally assisted dating has its roots in 1959, when two Stanford students used an IBM computer to match men and women based on punch-card questionnaires. Four decades later, the dating services we recognise today started appearing, with the launch of Match.com in 1995, soon followed by JDate (for Jewish singles), eHarmony and OKCupid. Fast-forward another 15 years and mobile apps such as Grindr and Tinder kicked online dating firmly into the smartphone era, introducing the idea of location-based matching and the now-ubiquitous 'swipe-right-for-yes, swipe-left-for-no' mechanism.

With hundreds of potential dates just a few taps away, it's never been easier to put yourself out there, but when it comes to matters of the heart there's no cheat code. Digital tools have brought new form to age-old anxieties, as well as giving rise to a whole new set of dating dilemmas. What is the etiquette of sexting? How can you slide into someone's DMs without looking like a sleazeball? Is ghosting ever OK? And what does any of that even mean?

Here we will navigate the perils and pitfalls of digital romance. It's a constantly evolving field, but while apps come and go and social mores shift, bear in mind that pretty much all relationship etiquette (digital or otherwise) ultimately boils down to two things: consent and reciprocity. Get those two covered and you can't go too far wrong. In short: don't be a creep.

ONLINE DATING

THERE ARE APPROXIMATELY one zillion dating sites and apps out there, from the sort that have enough mass-appeal to advertise on prime-time TV to those of a much more niche variety. Only interested in dating fellow vegans? Take your pick of plant-based matchmakers. Looking to satisfy your most peculiar fetish? There are places where your wildest kink will be considered thoroughly vanilla. Think you could only truly connect with someone who shares your passion for *Star Trek*? There are *multiple* Trekkie-specific dating sites.

Most dating services are open to all genders and sexual orientations, although many of the biggest names assume heterosexuality by default. Some, such as Grindr and HER, specifically target LGBTQI communities. It should go without saying, but do not try to hijack an app targeted at a community you're not part of. I'm looking at you, heterosexual guys:

stay off the lesbian profiles. If you're looking for a third-party 'unicorn' for your fantasy threesome, there are literally apps for that.

Different platforms have different reputations, and there's even evidence that people's behaviour changes with the weather, giving rise to a phenomenon known as 'cuffing season'. Nothing to do with leather and chains, cuffing season describes the time period from autumn through to spring, when the cold weather sets in and previously happy-go-lucky singletons find them-selves longing to couple up with someone to see through the winter. Suddenly, everyone you know seems to be settling down in a lovestruck hibernation. Once the frost thaws, however, it's back to business as usual: OKCupid reports an average 17 per cent increase in people looking for a one-night stand across April, May and June.

THE DATING PROFILE

WRITING A DATING profile is *hard*. Perhaps that's why so many people don't bother, leaving the text box either entirely blank or dashing off a few clichés that really say nothing at all. On the positive side, this means that it's really not difficult to be better than most other people.

Start with the basics. Think of your profile as a CV for romance: the aim is to make enough of an impression on paper that you get invited to an interview (or, in this case, on a date). You'll usually be asked to give your first name or a nickname. Don't add your surname; you don't want to make it too easy for any old internet stalker to find out your real identity. You'll also need to give some basic information such as your age, sex/

gender and location – 'a/s/l' as it was called in the olden days, when people still used chat rooms. *Do not lie about your age.* It's deceitful, it's sleazy, and it's hardly an auspicious start to a relationship if you're lying to someone before you've even met.

Some sites will ask for more specific information – *Are you religious? Are you a smoker? Do you like to be tied up in bed?* – and then there's usually a spot to write a brief personal bio. Keep it concise and upbeat. You're trying to make yourself look approachable; this is not the place for philosophical monologues, deep and meaningful chats, or your in-depth opinions on Brexit.

Here's a simple four-part template to get you started:

1. A catchy opener

This is your ice-breaker. Keep it short and sweet.

2. A description of yourself

This is basically your *Sleepless in Seattle* moment. You want to summarise who you are in just a few words – like 'Full-time barista, part-time bass-player' or 'Shy Northerner, new in town'.

Choose something that speaks specifically to the kind of person you are. Avoid listing generic positive traits; people will assume you're decent, kind and friendly unless you show them otherwise.

You don't really need to describe your personality – that's more easily done through actions than words – but if you want to give it a shot, stick to a maximum of two or three adjectives. A long list of character traits can easily be construed as just one: self-obsessed.

WHAT YOUR DATING BIO REALLY SAYS ABOUT YOU

'Confident' – *Loud*

'Mature' – *Boring*

'Old-Fashioned' – *Sexist*

'Adventurous' – *You did a gap year*

'Fun' – *Promiscuous*

'Introverted' – *Narcissistic*

'Ambitious' – *Workaholic*

'Spontaneous' – *Basic*

'Open-minded' – *Kinky*

'Creative' – *You work in marketing*

'Spiritual' – *You went to Burning Man once and like to tell everyone that it's 'not just an event, it's a state of mind'*

'Easygoing' – *You won't text back*

3. Your hobbies and interests

How you spend your time says a lot more about you than any self-description could. There's also another reason this section is important to include: it gives people something to latch on to when they first message you. As much as you're trying to give a sense of who you are, you're also offering up a ready-made ice-breaker, giving people the opportunity to say 'I like horror films too,' or 'What's the last sci-fi book you read?'

Again, make it specific. Literally everyone likes 'food, fun and travel' and you're helping no one with the classic 'I like going out and staying in.' It's more remarkable if you *don't* like coffee and pizza than if you do, and I refuse to believe that anyone feels *that* passionately about the Oxford comma.

A few examples will do; you're just trying to give a sense of your taste, not an encyclopaedic breakdown of your cultural psyche. Relationships are not made or broken on the back of the exact ranking of your top 10 punk records (as long as The Clash are in there somewhere).

On mobile apps, emoji are often used as shorthand for hobbies. If you're wondering why so many Tinder users seem to be keen gardeners, know that the leaf emoji usually implies an interest in marijuana, not rhododendrons.

4. What you're looking for

You don't want to present a list of demands, but you do want to indicate what sort of person you're hoping to meet and what sort of relationship you're after. Whether you're hoping to start an LTR ('long-term relationship') or are just DTF ('down to fuck') is totally fine – so long as the people you talk to are after the same thing. Things get a bit awkward when you're looking for a smutty hookup and they want someone to take home to their mother.

Keep it light; you don't want to scare people off. Something like, 'Looking to meet laid-back people for Netflix and chill,' or 'Hoping to find a like-minded person to share my life with' should adequately convey your intentions.

DECODING DATING ACRONYMS

Not sure what they're into? Here's a translation of some common dating site acronyms

BDSM – *bondage and discipline/dominance and submission/sadism and masochism, i.e. kink*

DTF – *down to fuck*

FWB – *friend with benefits*

LDR – *long-distance relationship*

LTR – *long-term relationship*

NSA – *no strings attached*

ONS – *one-night stand*

DATING PROFILE DON'TS

PERHAPS MORE IMPORTANT than what to put on your dating profile is what to avoid. There's nothing more disheartening than swiping through profile after profile and coming across the same cringeworthy bios again and again.

Maddie Holden, a lawyer and writer from New Zealand (and also the creator of the hilarious – and very NSFW – 'Critique my Dick Pic' Tumblr), was so disillusioned with the bios she saw while online dating that she started a side-hustle offering advice on people's profiles for $25 a pop. It all started when she was writing a guide to dating app Bumble for a men's lifestyle site and her editor asked her to take screenshots of some of the best examples of profiles she came across. 'I really struggled,' she says.

One of the most grievous mistakes, Holden adds, is what she calls the 'wish list' – when people rattle off a shopping list of traits their prospective match should or shouldn't have. Negative wish lists are the worst. 'Some women do this too,' she says, 'but it does seem to be more of a male trend, where they say, "I don't like girls who do duck face," or, "I don't like girls who use the Snapchat dog filter," or, "I'm not into women who wear too much make-up."' Entitled much? You're supposed to be selling yourself, not putting in an order at Dates 'R' Us.

Avoid the following faux pas and you're well on your way to a profile worthy of a swipe right.

Clichés

'Work hard, play harder.'

'It's not the destination, it's the journey.'

'Insert witty profile here.'

Cringe. Not forgetting the worst: 'Looking for a partner in crime.' Excuse me while I wipe the vomit off my phone screen.

Unoriginal jokes

The thing about jokes is they're supposed to be funny. Anyone who's spent more than ten minutes scrolling through a list of Tinder hopefuls will know that sinking feeling when you swipe right on someone you think has a great sense of humour – only to then see the same jokes repeated again and again in other people's profiles. You know the ones:

'Looking to leave the single market before the UK does.'

'I've got plenty of suits so I make a great +1 for weddings.'

'"Five stars!" – my mum.'

You might think you're coming across as a great wit, but really all you're saying is 'I'm so boring I had to google what to put in my dating app bio.'

Excuses about online dating

'Can't believe I'm on here.'

It's nearly 2020, love, we're all on here. How else do you expect to meet someone – in real life? Pervert.

Your height

The obsession with people featuring their height on their dating profiles truly baffles me. For many, it's the first attribute they list. Surely the fact you can reach the top shelf in Sainsbury's isn't your number one selling point? And if it is, perhaps you should get a hobby.

I've heard various justifications for including height, with straight men often complaining that they feel obliged to include theirs because women are only interested in men taller than them, and women complaining that *they* feel pressured to list theirs because men are only interested in women smaller than them. At this point, it seems that everyone is simply including it because everyone else does. While it's fine to have preferences, measuring someone's potential in feet and inches seems rather reductive to say the least (and no, putting something snarky like '6' 2" *seeing as everyone seems to care*' doesn't make you any better than the rest).

In any case, judging by all the men on dating sites who seem convinced that they're well over six foot, the numbers count for little. According to the Office for National Statistics, the average height for a man in the UK is five foot nine – so unless tall men are somehow more predisposed to use dating apps than the rest of the population, a lot of people are being rather liberal with the tape measure. In the US, OKCupid compared people's heights on their profiles to height distribution across the country, and concluded that both men and women exaggerate by about two inches.

You definitely don't need to give any other anatomical descriptions or, ahem, measurements. At least save it until you know each other well enough to private message.

Your Myers-Briggs personality type

Like many dating app users, I was initially puzzled by these strange acronyms peppering people's profiles. INTJ? ESFP? Were they secret societies? Some new dating slang, like the old GSOH ('good sense of humour') and WLTM ('would like to meet')?

No, these are Myers-Briggs types – the results of a popular personality test, most likely self-administered on a dodgy free website. The letters stand for different personality traits, with each one representing one option from a pair of characteristics: 'extraversion/introversion', 'sensing/intuition', 'thinking/feeling' and 'judging/perceiving'.

But although the test is popular among online daters, its scientific validity is questionable at best. Common criticisms include the fact that it relies on people giving objective assessments of themselves; that it forces people to categorise themselves in a binary way that doesn't reflect the breadth of human nature; and that the traits described are vague enough that they could feasibly apply to just about anyone – like a more intellectual-sounding horoscope.

And the thing is, even if you're confident that your Myers–Briggs type accurately reflects your personality, just listing those letters on your bio really doesn't say much. So you're an introvert who values intuition and thinking and prefers perception to judgement. What exactly is one of those when it's at home?

TMI

A final word of warning: remember that your dating profile will be visible to anyone else using the service, and it's not unlikely that could include people you know, such as coworkers, family members and ex-lovers. I once matched with someone on Tinder who bore a striking resemblance to a former flame – only to find out that he was, in fact, the same person. Reader, he had legally changed his name.

It's therefore best not to put anything on your public profile that you wouldn't want bringing up at the family dinner table or after-work drinks; save any particularly juicy details or personal proclivities for private chat.

And if you do come across someone you know and aren't interested in romantically, the best etiquette is to swipe left, move on, and *never, ever* mention it.

DATING APP PHOTOS

HOWEVER MUCH WORK you put into your bio, the thing that will catch people's eye first is your photo. It's easy to hand-wring about how online dating has turned us all into awful, shallow airheads who only care about looks, but really this isn't a fault of technology. We're visual creatures; don't try to tell me that if you were on a night out and looking to chat someone up, the first thing you'd notice would be their glowing personality.

And it's not just physical attraction. How someone looks can reveal a lot more about them. Consider all the cues we pick up on in real life, such as facial expressions, gestures and fashion sense. Do they have a genuine smile? Does their pose exude confidence, or do they seem more of the shy kind? Have they got good style, or are they the kind of person who still wears their hair in curtains, 20 years after the Backstreet Boys reached their peak?

First things first: you want a clear and accurate (i.e. recent) image that shows your face. Make sure it's decent quality – there's no excuse for a grainy or blurry photo when everyone's walking around with a high-spec camera in their pocket – and put some effort into it. Take a few minutes to tidy up whatever's in the background and check the lighting is flattering. Don't use flash, it adds years.

Most dating platforms will let you add multiple photos. Make them varied. Think one headshot, one full-body picture, and a few images that show you in whatever you consider to be your natural environment. The general consensus is that shirt-less pics are a no, smiles are a yes, and you should limit yourself to one or two selfies at most.

The Tinder school of portraiture

The rise of dating apps has inspired a whole new movement in photography. Here's a brief guide to some of the more prominent artistic trends:

The cute animal picture

If you get close enough to something cute, it'll rub off on you, right? That seems to be the logic behind the cute animal picture, which features the subject holding a puppy, kitten or other miscellaneous fluffy thing. And to be fair, it's not exactly wrong.

The gym selfie

The gym selfie has a strictly defined aesthetic: shot in the mirror, shirtless or wearing only a sports bra, with the subject's flexed abs taking up the majority of the frame. Sometimes their head isn't even in shot. Once you've seen a couple of these, you've seen them all. Yawn.

The bathroom selfie

You've just touched up your make-up and you've caught a glimpse of yourself in the mirror looking pretty fine, if you say so yourself. I get it, sometimes bathrooms have really good lighting. Just make sure the background's reasonably tidy. If the loo is in shot, it's an instant swipe left.

The Where's Wally? group shot

This is a classic: the shot of four or five people, any one of whom could be the person in the profile. The idea behind the group shot is presumably to prove that you're a person who has friends, and who has fun with their friends. What a friendly, fun person you must be! If you're lucky, someone might even confuse you with your better-looking mate . . .

The 'They're siblings, right?' double portrait

A pared-back version of the group shot, this photo shows the subject just a bit to close to someone else. They might have their arm around them, or be looking into their eyes. You're not sure if it's a sibling or an ex, but either way, it's a weird photo to pick. Just as bad is the picture that's clearly been cropped to cut someone – almost definitely an ex this time – out of the frame. Awkward.

The wedding guest portrait

Someone once told you you looked good in a suit, so here we are. You're hoping people might think you have some kind of flash job that means you always dress like this, but the floral buttonhole gives it away. You think you look like James Bond, but in reality, you're more Johnny English.

The look-how-good-I-am-with-kids picture

This idea comes from a similar place as the cute animal picture, but with very different results. Including pictures of children on your dating profile, in any context, is just creepy. Think about it: you're trying to use your kids to pull strangers on the internet. Or worse: you're trying to use *someone else's* kids to pull strangers on the internet.

The exotic animal picture

What you're trying to say with this is that you're totally into nature and saving the tigers and stuff. What you're *actually* saying is that you went to some questionable 'sanctuary' to pose with a probably drugged wild animal and all you thought about was how worldly it would make you look on your dating profile.

FINDING A MATCH, AND WHY YOU SHOULD MAKE THE FIRST MOVE

Now you've set up your profile and you're ready to start finding your next digital squeeze. First, a note on how dating sites work. You might think that, when you use a dating service, you're getting shown all the potential matches that meet your criteria, but this isn't usually the case. Here's the problem: if you let everyone pick and choose from everyone else, then you'll end up with some people who are extremely popular and some who are very unpopular. At one end of the spectrum, the very popular people will be inundated with messages; at the other, the least popular people will be left with empty inboxes. For both, the service becomes unusable.

As a result, most dating services use data analysis to figure out how popular each user is, and then match them with users of a similar popularity. The more popular you are, the more popular people you'll be matched with. Tinder allegedly calls this a person's 'Elo score', named after a rating system used to rank the skill level of chess players.

On some dating services, you can start messaging people straight off the bat. On others, you have to both express an interest, or 'match', before you can message. In a straight context, there's a huge imbalance between how men and women generally approach this. Men often play a numbers game, matching with as many women as possible, while women tend to be more picky, only matching with people they actually fancy. The irony is that, the more widespread these behaviours become, the more they reinforce the other: if men swipe right on everyone, women feel they have to be more selective so as to avoid being overwhelmed with matches. But if women only occasionally swipe right, men feel they have to be even more gung-ho with their swiping to increase their odds of getting a match.

There's a similar gender imbalance when it comes to first messages. Generally speaking, straight women send very few first messages and straight men send a lot more. This no doubt harks back to old-fashioned gender stereotypes about who should make the first move, but it doesn't do anyone any favours. Again, you end up with women swamped with messages and men frustrated at their lack of replies.

Dating app Bumble tries to address this problem by forcing women to message men first. But on all apps, it's advantageous to make the first move. Dale Markowitz, a software engineer and former data scientist at OKCupid, explains that whoever messages first is more likely to get their preferences in a partner and make less of a compromise. That's because the person who messages first essentially takes their pick of who they want to date. The person on the receiving end, meanwhile, may well respond to someone who meets most of their criteria but not all of them. 'In a way, whoever sends the first message has an advantage, in that what they want is who they end up dating,' she says. As men send so many more first messages (on OKCupid, men start around 80 per cent of conversations), they end up establishing the dating paradigm.

Take age, for example: there's lots of evidence out there that men tend to prefer dating younger women. But do women prefer dating older men? While at OKCupid, Markowitz looked at thousands of heterosexual interactions to investigate this age gap. She found that in over half of successful conversations ('successful conversations' being counted as threads that lasted for at least four messages), the man was older than the woman. When she looked more closely at how people directed their messages, however, she found that men tended to message younger women but women tended to message men closer to their own age. And as women got older, they actually responded more often to younger men.[3]

This, concludes Markowitz, suggests that the age gap may be driven more by men's preferences than women's; if more women took the initiative to message their ideal dates, then perhaps the dynamic would shift. And when women do put themselves out there, they can flip the norms. Markowitz found that a 40-year-old woman was actually more likely to get a response from a 25-year-old than a 55-year-old man. Admittedly, this may be partly down to the novelty, given it is currently unusual for women to message first – but it's a heartening reminder that you can't get what you don't ask for. So don't be shy; go ahead and make the first move.

The first message

'Hey' won't cut it. Neither will its more provocative cousin 'Heyy' (there's something so salacious about that extra 'y', isn't there?). Such a lazy message is unlikely to get you a response, and if it does, it'll probably just be another 'Hey' back – which puts you right back at square one.

Pick-up lines are universally terrible, as are inane questions about whether you'd rather fight one horse-sized duck or 100 duck-sized horses, or whatever other nonsense. And yes, we've all heard the one about the *Titanic* – 'it broke the ice.' (Although, when you think about it, didn't the ice break the Titanic?)

Putting together a decent first message isn't rocket science. You can break it down into a simple formula:

Positive reference to thing on their profile + question = decent chance of success

For example:

'Cute dog! How old is he?'

'Great to meet another horror film fan. What's the last one you watched?'

'Nice Statue of Liberty picture. When were you in New York?'

By following this formula you're doing two things: proving you've actually looked at their profile and aren't just copy-pasting the same message to everyone, and making it as easy as possible for them to respond.

Be nice, but avoid empty compliments, especially on someone's appearance – in a first message, this comes across as at best inauthentic and at worst just sleazy. Hit send, and then the ball's in their court. If they don't respond, you can follow up once, but that's it. After that, take the hint and move on. As they say, there are plenty of fish in the sea – or, indeed, on Plenty of Fish.

Transitioning from online to IRL

Most people aren't on dating apps to find a pen pal and, after a few successful messages, you probably want to float the idea of a meeting. There's something to be said for the chemistry you feel (or don't feel) when meeting in person that simply can't be captured in messages, and you don't want to invest too heavily in someone who turns out to have really bad body odour or terrible table manners, or who spends the whole date talking about how, seriously, their startup is *so close* to making it really big.

Take a few simple precautions before meeting your date. Google them beforehand and check out their social media to make sure there aren't any obvious red flags. Choose a neutral location for your first meeting and let a friend know in advance where you're going and when you expect to be back. It's a good idea to set a fixed end time to the date when you first arrange it, so that you have an easy out should things get awkward or the chemistry just isn't there.

DANGEROUS DATING BEASTS AND HOW TO AVOID THEM

I T'S A JUNGLE out there. Here are some of the invasive species that have made online dating their habitat – and that are best kept at a distance.

The catfish

The catfish is quite literally too good to be true. Lurking in the shallows of any dating app, they pull you in with a tempting photo and winning bio. Message for any amount of time, however, and you'll start to see inconsistencies in their story. They seem rather coy about sharing more photos and even more reluctant to talk on Skype or meet in person. A reverse-image search reveals their pictures are attached to a Facebook profile under someone else's name or appear on a stock photo website. Eventually, you find out that Claudia the part-time model is actually Klaus, the bored teenager.

The Intellectual

The Intellectual is not just someone who's a bit bookish, but someone who will tell you in complete earnestness that they consider themselves to be An Intellectual (and will expect you to be impressed). They find creative ways to drop their IQ score into casual conversation and will never use an everyday word when they can find a barely used synonym instead. *You're not just beautiful, darling, you're positively pulchritudinous!* Other giveaways include: any mention of quantum physics, listing their sexuality as 'sapiosexual' and a general scorn for popular culture (except for their favourite TV show, which is either *The Big Bang Theory* or *Rick and Morty*).

The married man

Or woman. But usually man. For the most part, the married man lists himself as single and targets younger women. Alternatively, he might put something like 'it's complicated', or insist that he's 'poly', or 'in an open relationship' (helpful reminder: cheating isn't the same as polyamory, and it only counts as an open relationship if your partner agrees). In rare cases, the married man is upfront about his marital status – and then tries to sell you a sob story about the loveless life that only you can save him from. In reality, he probably has no interest in leaving his spouse and will most likely bottle it before he even gets as far as an affair. The attention is an ego-boost, but as soon as things get too real, *poof!* He's ghosted.

The Nice Guy

A well-documented online phenomenon, the Nice Guy is anything but. Nice Guys believe that the reason they can't get a girlfriend is no fault of their own; the problem is that women just can't see what a great catch they are. A Nice Guy's only foible, you see, is that he's 'too nice', and 'nice guys finish last'. Women *say* they want nice guys, the Nice Guy whines, but really they go for jerks. This leaves the Nice Guy firmly relegated to the mythical 'friend zone' – and why would a nice guy like him want to be your *friend?* The Nice Guy promises that he's not like other guys; he'll treat you right, m'lady. Unless it turns out that you're not sexually attracted to him, in which case, he was just joking – *as if he'd ever be interested in you, you fat slut!*

The 'not like other girls' girl

Similar to the Nice Guy, the 'not like other girls' girl takes great pains to show off how different and quirky she is – *not like all those other girls.* She turns her nose up at anything stereotypically feminine and thinks she's a special snowflake for liking video games, drinking beer or having tattoos. She wants you to know that she could totally just chill out with your guy friends – she's cool like that. The problem with the 'not like other girls' girl is that her whole schtick relies on false and harmful stereotypes about what 'other girls' are like, when in reality they are of course all individuals with their own stuff going on. In that respect, the 'not like other girls' girl is, ironically, exactly like other girls.

The modern misogynist

If only the Nice Guy was as bad as it got. Unfortunately, the internet has become home to a frightening range of misogynistic communities that can be quite extreme in their hatred of women. These online groups are all slightly different in their ideologies but share the same basic belief that men and women are fundamentally different. Often homophobic and racist to boot, they are nostalgic for traditional gender roles and think that feminism has 'gone too far'. They feel entitled to sex – but only with women they deem attractive enough, of course – and can get aggressive and even violent if denied. These tragic men might inspire pity, if it weren't for the fact they're so utterly vile.

TELLTALE SIGNS TO HELP YOU SPOT – AND AVOID – THE MODERN MISOGYNIST:

- Refers to macho men as 'alphas' and others as 'betas'
- Has *The Game* by Neil Strauss on his bookshelf
- Takes an inordinate amount of pride in going to the gym
- Tries to 'neg' you – a kind of backhanded compliment aimed at undermining a person's confidence to make them more vulnerable ('You'd be pretty if you had better teeth,' 'Nice hair, is it fake?')
- Takes great interest in evolutionary biology and refers to human relationships in weirdly biological terms, like calling sex 'mating'
- Calls women 'females'

- Is adamant that misandry is a thing
- Worships Jordan Peterson
- Has no platonic female friends
- Calls men who do have female friends 'white knights' or 'social justice warriors'
- Describes sexual experiences in such great detail it's almost as if he made them up. . .
- Gaslights you when you try to question any of the above

THE NEW RULES OF FLIRTING

REGARDLESS OF WHETHER you meet someone online or the old-fashioned way, relationships today are conducted at least partly through digital lines of communication. Where we once agonised over the punctuation in a handwritten love letter, so we now sigh over the little electronic ticks that tell us a love interest has seen our latest message but not yet deemed it worthy of a response.

I had a girl friend at school who, when it came to flirting with boys, used to insist on following 'The Rules' – a kind of dating code based on the 1995 book of the same name by Ellen Fein and Sherrie Schneider. These 'Rules' (which, as you can probably guess, were rather outdated and very sexist) essentially revolved around making yourself appear mysterious and elusive, of 'playing hard to get'. This friend used to make guys wait two days – *days!* – before texting them back.

Today, if a love interest kept me waiting more than a few

hours for a reply, I'd probably assume they were either no longer interested, ghosting me or lying dead in a ditch.

Playing games is not usually consistent with good etiquette, leading as it does only to frustration on all sides. If you want to text someone back, text them back. Leaving them waiting is just rude and shows a disregard for their time (see also Chapter 3: 'Left on Read').

That said, you don't want to overdo your affections to the point that you become a nag. When it comes to romantic messaging, more important than timing or frequency is *reciprocity*. Are they texting back as much as you are? Are they responding with the same level of intimacy, or have their messages devolved into the occasional 'hmm' and 'haha'? It takes two to flirt. Next, we shall delve into some of the dating behaviours specific to digital platforms.

SIGNS THEY'RE PROBABLY INTO YOU

They like all your social media posts

They particularly like your selfies

They respond to your messages instantly

They laugh (or LOL) at your jokes

They send you cute animal memes or gifs

They text first thing in the morning/last thing at night

They never break your Snapchat streak

They watch all your Instagram Stories

They use the winky face emoji when they message you

Breadcrumbing

Breadcrumbing is a phenomenon whereby a person sends you just enough messages to keep your attention while having no real intention of moving forward with a relationship. The breadcrumber has a sixth sense for when you're about to lose interest and hooks you back with a flirtatious message, hinting that things could go further – before disappearing again. What they're after is attention; they like the ego-boost of feeling that they *could* have something with you, even though they're not actually into it. They're wasting your time.

Sliding into DMs

The DM slide is a classic move. Sliding into DMs describes when you transition from public social media interactions to a private chat, with flirtatious intentions. Or, as the top definition on Urban Dictionary puts it, 'When you start a direct message chain on Facebook, Instagram, or Twitter, with the hopes of acquiring the booty.' One minute you're liking and commenting on someone's public posts, the next you're sending them a direct message. It's called 'sliding' because the instigator usually hopes to pull off this segue seamlessly and come out of it looking incredibly smooth. In reality, this is rarely the case.

Sliding into DMs has earned the reputation of being a bit of a sleazy move, largely due to the speed with which many DM-sliders manage to jump from hello to harassment. That said, it is possible to pull it off without being a total creep. The key, as ever, is context. A good DM slide should not happen out of the blue; you need to work up to it. 'Just as it would be very invasive in real life for someone to come up to you and start talking to you non-stop, you have to pick up on social cues and pick up on their interest,' says Taylor Lorenz, a journalist who writes about internet culture for the *Atlantic*.

Imagine it like this: you're chatting to a group of people in real life, in a public place. You catch someone's eye, and perhaps join in a conversation in shared company. Later, you find an opportunity to talk to them one-on-one, in the hope of making a move. This is the real-world equivalent of the DM slide and, like its digital cousin, it can either be the start of a beautiful relationship or a thoroughly mortifying experience that you'd rather never think about again.

The best way to lay the groundwork for romance over social media is to start by liking some of your crush's posts. Keep an eye out for a response – are they liking your posts in return? If so, try advancing to a comment here and there before building up to the direct message.

If you're a man sliding into a woman's DMs, remember that her experience of the internet is likely to be very different to yours, and she may (justifiably) be suspicious of your intentions. Lorenz says that she has had so many problems with men sending her unwanted messages on Twitter that she now just tells everyone she doesn't do DMs. Her advice: 'I would tell women to put themselves out there a little bit more in terms of engaging with new people online and initiating messages, and I would tell men to cool it and triple-guess everything you do, because you're probably being annoying to someone.'

Tindstagramming

Tindstagramming is the creepier cousin of the DM slide. This is when someone swipes right on your profile on Tinder but you swipe left, meaning you don't 'match' and they can't message you. But instead of taking the rejection on the chin like a grown-up, they track you down on Instagram and message you there instead.

Tindstagramming is always unacceptable. If someone hasn't replied to your advances on a dating app, you can take that as a resounding 'no'. Don't make them turn you down twice.

Deep-liking

'Deep-liking' can happen to the best of us, but that doesn't stop it being excruciating every time. This is when you're casually lurking on your date's social media profiles, trawling through all their photos – and then accidentally hit 'like' on a picture of them from six years ago, thus revealing yourself to be the creepy stalker we all are when it comes to our online crushes. Mortifying.

It's hard to come back from a deep-like. Your best bet is to immediately unlike and hope against hope that they didn't notice. If they did, then – well, I suppose you could always leave social media, vow to remain single for ever, and go and live the rest of your life off-grid in a forest somewhere?

If you're on the receiving end of a deep-like, take it as a compliment, and bask in the relief that it happened to them, not you.

Sexting

You've done your flirting, your partner's into it, and now you're ready to turn up the heat. Sexting – sending sexually explicit messages, photos or videos – is an increasingly popular pastime. A 2016 study led by Justin Garcia at the Kinsey Institute, Indiana University, found that 21 per cent of single Americans surveyed had sent sexually explicit messages, with younger respondents more likely to have done so.[4]

As with any sexual activity, at the heart of sexting etiquette is consent. You should have no doubt before you send someone an explicit message that they actually want to receive it. If you're not sure, ask. It might feel mildly embarrassing, but much less so than dealing with the consequences of sending an unwanted sext. Just spit it out: *'Can I send you some sexy messages?'* Add a winky face emoji if you must.

Once you've got (enthusiastic) consent, the real challenge starts: being sexy over the internet. We'll start with sexting by text, the natural continuation of old-school phone sex. This can include anything from risqué compliments to transcribed role-play (*'Ooh, I'm taking off my bra. . .' 'I'm caressing your inner thigh. . .'*)

Writing sex is notoriously difficult. Some of literature's greatest minds (as well as former Smiths frontman Morrissey) have found themselves lampooned at the *Literary Review*'s annual Bad Sex in Fiction Award for sex scenes that are anything but arousing. Their problem is usually trying to be too creative – think 'bulbous salutations' and barrel-rolling breasts (and those are just Morrissey). Luckily, you're not trying to win any literary prizes with your sexts. Embrace the clichés, find what works for you both, and don't even think about reaching for the thesaurus. If you're not sure where to start, try referencing your last meeting or describing what you want to do when you next see each other.

Different strokes for different folks, but it's often the case that less is more. 'In general, people miss a step in thinking that sexting is about the actual sex,' says Lea Robinson, a writer who has published more than 100 erotic novels together with co-author Melissa King under the pseudonym Alexa Riley. The secret to hot dirty talk, she says, is in the promise of what's to come. King agrees: 'It's not the actual sex, it's everything that builds up to it.'

Sexy emoji

If you're struggling to use your words, just say it in emoji. There are no emoji specifically designed for sex (except perhaps the 'love hotel'), but, being the immature humans that we are, we have developed a whole set of double-entendres for the most innocent of icons. To get those with the highest potential for embarrassing misunderstandings out of the way first: the aubergine emoji is pretty much only ever used in modern messaging to represent a penis, and the peach is almost never the fruit and almost always a nice ripe derrière.

EMOJI SEXTING TRANSLATION GUIDE

From the mildly suggestive to the full-on full-frontal, here are some popular emoji euphemisms:

Winking face – flirtatious wink

Smirking face – 'Let's get it on'

Aubergine – penis

Peach – bum

Water droplets – bodily fluids of any description

Pointing fingers – touching

Waving hand – spanking

Closed fist – hand job

Tongue or face with tongue sticking out – oral

Champagne bottle/fireworks/confetti/rocket/explosion – climax

Blushing face – post-coital glow

Other emoji can also take on lewd meanings depending on context, such as the disembodied tongue or the water droplets – which are technically meant to be sweat but could conceivably convey other bodily fluids. You can even link emoji together in sequences to represent complete sex acts, as in the rather X-rated expression of self-love, *closed fist – aubergine – water droplets*.

Interestingly, there is no universally accepted emoji for the vulva or vagina, and though you could attempt to convey this creatively – perhaps with the cat emoji; the taco; or the tulip, Georgia O'Keeffe style – it's unlikely people would immediately understand what you meant, and very likely to be 50 shades of awkward.

Sending nudes

When people talk about sexting these days, they're often not referring to texted sweet nothings but to explicit photos. The phrase 'send nudes' has become a common internet meme, and can be used both as an earnest request and a punchline to jokes.

As ever, the most important thing to consider when exchanging nudes is consent. Sending someone nudes *with consent* can be hot, charming and part of an ordinary, healthy relationship. Sending the same pictures without consent is really no better than flashing someone in the street – gross, pervy and potentially illegal. Take note, unsolicited dick pic senders: no one wants to see your privates unless they explicitly tell you they want to. Just because a woman is so presumptuous as to be active on the internet does not mean she is fair game for your icky photos.

If you do have consent, ask yourself one other important question: do you trust the person you're sharing images with

to respect your privacy? You need to be aware that any images you put online could end up travelling further than you expect. Sending nudes has become particularly popular on 'ephemeral' apps like Snapchat, where messages disappear after being read, but even here, the recipient can screenshot or otherwise make a copy without your knowledge.

Ann Olivarius, a lawyer who specialises in fighting for women's rights, warns about 'revenge porn' – a term that describes when someone (often a vengeful ex) shares explicit images without your permission, for example posting them on social media or messaging them to other people. 'Usually when people are about to do this, they don't stop and think, "What if he takes these pictures and puts them on the internet when we break up?"' she says.

You can't stop someone from being a future jerk, but you can take a few mitigating precautions, such as keeping your face out of shot so you can't be easily identified if the picture falls into malicious hands. Before you send a picture to someone, it's a good idea to also clarify that it's intended for their eyes only, to make sure you're on the same page. As a recipient, you should treat other people's nudes with the utmost of confidence. If you break up, delete them.

MAKING THINGS OFFICIAL

IN THE OLDEN days (the early noughties), you knew a relationship was the real deal when it became *Facebook official*. Forget meeting their parents or opening a joint bank account; if you weren't marked 'in a relationship with' someone on your Facebook profile, then you couldn't be truly serious about it.

Nowadays, listing your relationship on Facebook seems rather passé, but that doesn't mean you can ignore your significant other on social media. *Atlantic* writer Taylor Lorenz believes that engaging with a loved one's online content – whether that's on Instagram, Twitter, Snapchat, or anywhere else – is an essential part of modern relationships. 'I think that online relationships should mimic your real-life relationship as closely as possible,' she says. 'If you're spending a lot of time with your significant other in real life and they're nowhere on your social media, that's a bit weird.'

Lorenz has written about the trend of 'going Instagram official' on her Medium site.[5] Going Instagram official essentially means coming out with your relationship on the platform, usually by posting a picture of you both looking cute together with a corny caption or some heart emojis. Related behaviour includes 'twinstagramming' (posting pictures from the same place at the same time) and 'subgramming' (posting pictures or

MODERN LOVE IS . . .

. . . liking every post

. . . never leaving them on read

. . . having 'our' emoji

. . . going social media official

. . . texting them even though your battery's at 5%

. . . taking 100 photos to get their best Instagram shot

. . . trusting them with your Netflix password

. . . saving their address on Deliveroo because you're there so often captions that seem innocuous to an outsider but have a special meaning for their intended viewer). 'Instagram official is basically how everybody declares their relationship now,' Lorenz says.

Marriage in the age of social media

Call me old-fashioned, but certain major relationship milestones should remain analogue. Proposals should be made in person, wedding invitations should be sent on paper, and most stag and hen party photos are really best left off the internet. That's not to say that social media has no place in romantic events. Used correctly, it can be a great way to share these special moments with family and friends.

Let's start with proposals. These should be kept intimate. Personally, I can't think of anything worse than a choreographed dance flash mob, or anything else that might have the chance of 'going viral'. If you want to film the moment for posterity, keep it low-key; you don't want your partner to feel even more on-the-spot than they already are.

Proposal over and accepted, it's perfectly acceptable to announce the engagement on social media, should you so wish. Judging by the activity of my Facebook friends, there is one way and one way only in which you may do this: a photo of the bride-to-be's hand wrapped around a champagne glass, with their ring finger on prominent display and the caption 'She said yes!'

Tell your close family and friends before posting; they deserve the personal touch. Never post about someone else's engagement on social media without their approval, as they may not yet have had the chance to share the news.

When it comes to the wedding, the main point of contention

is usually photos. Some couples encourage guests to take pictures for social media and tag them with a cheesy hashtag, while others ask for an 'unplugged' wedding and for photography to be left to the professionals. Others request that guests refrain from taking pictures during the ceremony itself or ask that they are not posted online until later.

As a guest, you should respect the couple's wishes. If in doubt, assume that no photos are to be posted until after the ceremony has concluded and the party is in full swing. Absolutely do not post any pictures of the bride getting ready before the ceremony unless you have her permission; you don't want to ruin her big reveal.

If you're part of the happy couple, you'll no doubt want to share your wedding photos with the world. The etiquette here boils down to one thing: don't be insufferable. Remember that, while it may have been the happiest day of your life, to many of your social media connections it's just one more wedding appearing in their feed. Making too much of a fuss can appear obnoxious, especially to single friends.

Pick the best photos and upload them together; don't dripfeed them out in an extended trawl for likes. You may permit yourself one or two #throwback posts in the year directly following the wedding, but after that you should hold off for anniversaries.

BREAKING UP

THE ONE THING more difficult than starting a relationship is ending one, and digital reminders can make it tough to move on from a past love. It's easy to fall into the trap of stalking your ex's social media feeds to see what they're up to (and with whom), but in all likelihood this will only make you feel more miserable. If you know you have a tendency to wallow, it's best to just unfollow and unfriend an ex, at least until the wound has healed somewhat.

Ghosting

Ghosting refers to the heart-wrenching moment when someone ends a relationship by simply stopping responding to messages. One minute you're chatting away, the next – poof! – they've disappeared without a digital trace.

Ghosting isn't an entirely new phenomenon, but modern technology has made it more widespread. If your relationship is conducted heavily through messaging and social media, it's a lot easier to drop off the map. Relationship counsellor Peter Saddington says one reason ghosting may have become more common is because relationships developed over digital platforms can get very close very fast. 'When couples start their relationship and spend a lot of time texting each other, the level of intimacy they achieve is quicker than, say, meeting face to face,' he explains. 'As a consequence, I think people can be tempted into forming relationships – getting very intense, very deep – and then starting to get cold feet when somebody says something or does something to put them off.'

Ghosting usually comes from a place of shame and embarrassment: it's the easy way out when you don't have the guts to tell someone you're just not into them any more. But for the ghosted, it can be devastating. 'Somehow it feels incredibly disrespectful and hurtful – as if you're not taken into account as a true human being,' Saddington says.

There are some truly awful examples out there. In an

article for Mashable, journalist Rachel Thompson recalled a time she met someone on dating app Hinge and got as far as ordering a drink at the restaurant they'd agreed to meet at before being ghosted. She noticed that her WhatsApp messages asking her date where he was had not gone through – they only had one tick next to them instead of two, indicating that he had blocked her number. When she checked the Hinge app, he was no longer in her matches. After speaking to other people who had been similarly stood up, she came up with the term 'cloaking' to describe this particularly heinous type of last-minute ghosting – 'given that these people essentially don an invisibility cloak after setting up a date'.[6]

Her experience was at least possibly better than one poor soul on Twitter, however, who tweeted that she'd been seeing someone for around three months before he ghosted her, only for him to later match with her again on Tinder. He sent a message with five words: 'You should get yourself tested.' He didn't respond to follow-up messages.[7]

It's perfectly reasonable to want to end a relationship, but you need to actually end it – don't just leave things hanging. If you've been seeing someone for a while, you should buck up and tell them to their face. If it's a more casual arrangement, it's fine to do it over messaging, but make your intentions clear.

Instead of ghosting, journalist, broadcaster and sex educator Alix Fox suggests that you should 'casper'. Named after the friendly ghost, caspering involves sending one last message to explain that you don't want to continue the relationship, and *then* ghosting. 'Try and leave them something constructive,' Fox advises. 'Give them the dignity and closure of a final statement saying that you are cutting them off, so you don't leave them hanging, wondering what they did wrong.'

She suggests something along the lines of: *'Hey, I don't think we're a good match, so I'm going to move on. It's been really nice when you've thoughtfully asked me how my days have been, so thank you. Good luck for the future.'*

That way, you get your clean break, but they get to move on as well, without wondering if you've been hit by a bus.

There are, of course, exceptions. 'If someone has been wildly inappropriate or a complete asshole, then by all means ghost them,' she says. 'In that case, it's a righteous ghosting.'

DIGITAL CURES FOR HEARTBREAK

- Head to your friends' WhatsApp group to commiserate about how you deserve better and they were never good enough for you anyway.

- Treat yourself to a 'Netflix and chill' night where you actually just watch Netflix and chill.

- Go through the ritual of unfollowing and unfriending them on all social media platforms. For that extra feeling of smugness, block them too.

- Call your mum.

- Make a new Spotify playlist of your favourite upbeat songs.

- Browse Reddit's r/aww forum for an endless stream of cute animal pics; make one your phone wallpaper.

- Create an online dating profile and enjoy the ego boost when people match with you, even if you're not quite ready to move on just yet.

- Ask a friend to do an Instagram shoot of you looking cute and update your profile picture.

- Like and leave positive comments on mutual friends' social media posts to show how totally fine you're doing.

LEFT ON READ

THE ART OF FRIENDSHIP

FIVE GOLDEN RULES

1. Never leave a friend on read

2. Messaging means conversation, not monologue

3. What happens in the group chat stays in
the group chat

4. No one likes an unexpected phone call

5. Friends don't phub friends

Before mobile phones, friendship was defined by long chats on the landline. You'd know your best friend's number by heart, call whenever you fancied a chat and spend whole evenings gossiping down the receiver. Today, the prospect of an unexpected phone call from anyone is frankly rather alarming, and another technology has come to define modern friendship: the messaging app.

My experience of messaging is similar to that of most Millennials. It started with SMS on a pay-as-you-go Nokia 3510, where every message was carefully crafted to fit as many words into one text as possible, so as not to cost more credit. Everyone became an expert in 'text speak', eking as much out of the 160-character limit as possible so that evry msg lookd smthg lyk ths. Now, messaging is almost entirely conducted through smartphone apps such as WhatsApp and iMessage, which use Wi-Fi or cellular data instead of the SMS protocol, and which let you type a hell of a lot of emojis before getting anywhere near a character limit.

As if chatting one-on-one didn't pose enough etiquette dilemmas, these apps have also introduced a way of communicating with entire friendship circles at once: the group chat. At their best, group chats can bring people together, connecting friends across time and distance and putting a 24-hour support group at your fingertips. At their worst, they can see you waking up to another 200+ notifications from that WhatsApp group you joined as part of a hen do six months ago and are now trapped in forever, fearing you'll cause mortal offence should you leave.

In this chapter, we'll look at messaging, the group chat, the phone call (gulp), and the digital etiquette of everyday conversation in these brave new media. Our friends may just be a couple of taps away, but while it's never been easier to reach them, it can be harder than ever to say the right thing – to the point that we've even developed whole new ways of speaking (or writing) in order to get our messages across. Because nothing says 'I love you, buddy' like a perfectly timed gif.

THE MESSAGING APP

MESSAGING HAS BECOME the de facto medium for chatting with friends because of its conversational nature. It's faster and friendlier than email, and less intrusive than an unexpected phone call. More importantly, it's instant (or about as close as you can get), which means it's perfect for in-the-moment discussions, where fast responses mimic the immediacy of a face-to-face chat.

As such, the key to good messaging is the same as good conversation. You should be having a back-and-forth discussion, not delivering a monologue. Messages should be kept short – a couple of sentences at the most – and written off the cuff. An informal tone is not only acceptable but often required. As with email, if you have to stop and think about it too much before sending, you're probably in the wrong place; maybe you should be talking in person.

Given the quick-fire nature of messaging, a key point of its etiquette is the prompt response. You might not necessarily

MESSAGING APP HOROSCOPE: WHAT YOUR DEFAULT MESSENGER SAYS ABOUT YOU

WhatsApp

You don't overcomplicate things. You're totally normal.

Facebook Messenger

You still actively update your Facebook status. You're probably over 40.

Signal

Your friends describe you as smart, techy and a little paranoid. You like wearing black hoodies. Your favourite topic of discussion is telling everyone why you're not on Facebook.

Snapchat

You're still in full-time education. Selfies make up more than 50 per cent of the total number of pictures stored on your phone.

Instagram DMs

You're also young, but you think that Snapchat was, like, *sooo* last year.

Twitter DMs

You work in media.

Something else

Well look at you, you quirky little cookie.

have your phone on you at all times, but you're bound to check it at least every few hours (and let's not kid ourselves, it's probably closer to every few minutes). Don't leave a friend hanging. A fast response with the occasional typo will almost always be more appreciated than a witty reply delivered hours later.

This is especially true if you are part-way through a conversation. You wouldn't suddenly stop mid-way through talking to someone in real life, so don't do it here either. There's nothing worse than being in the middle of some juicy gossip and suddenly getting blanked, so that you're compelled to keep checking your phone every 30 seconds just in case you didn't hear it buzz. If you need to duck out of a chat before it's come to its natural end, simply send a quick note saying as much, and resume the discussion when you're able to.

There are dozens of messaging apps out there, most of which have very similar functionality, though they may emphasise different features or appeal to different demographics. Just make sure you join one that your friends actually use too, or it rather defeats the purpose. When I downloaded Snapchat in my late 20s, excited to share dog-filter selfies with all my contacts on the app, I was met with nothing but digital tumbleweed and a cruel reminder of the inexorable march of time.

READ RECEIPTS, OR THE INIMITABLE
TORTURE OF BEING LEFT ON READ

IF PROMPT REPLIES are the first rule of messaging etiquette, leaving someone 'on read' represents the ultimate faux pas.

Read receipts, or the 'seen function', are the little signifiers that let you know someone has read your message. On

Facebook Messenger, for instance, a little white circle with a blue tick means your message has been sent, a blue circle with a white tick means it's been delivered, and a miniature icon of your recipient's profile picture means it has been read. On WhatsApp, one grey tick means your message has been sent; two grey ticks mean your message has been received; and two blue ticks mean your message has been read. (Note that read receipts are different to *delivery* receipts, which only tell you your message has been delivered, not read.)

This mechanism is ostensibly a handy little feature to let you know when someone's available to talk, but, more often than not, all it does is lead to that singular and exquisite agony: being *left on read.*

Being left on read – or, as it's sometimes known, being 'blue-ticked' – is when you can see that someone has read your message, but they haven't replied. You can witness the rejection before your very eyes. You send a message, you watch the little icons change colour, you see them turn to 'read' . . . and then, nothing. Those two little blue ticks are just left hanging. Your message has been read and ignored, deemed unworthy of response.

The anxiety, anger and shame that come with being left on read can be brutal. It's not that the person hasn't responded that hurts; it's that you know they have *chosen* not to respond. Those little blue ticks cruelly strip you of the lies you could otherwise tell yourself as to why they're not messaging back. *Maybe they don't have their phone on them, maybe they didn't see the message, maybe they're just too busy.* You *know* they saw the message. You *know* they have their phone on them. You *know* they had time enough to open the message.

Of course, there's usually a perfectly boring and reasonable explanation as to why someone hasn't immediately responded to your message after reading. Perhaps they got distracted. Perhaps they don't know the answer to a question you asked and plan to get back to you later. Perhaps they checked your message because they thought it might be something important, but actually you were just sharing a link to a funny YouTube video and really they have more important things to do right now, OK?

But these aren't the explanations your brain entertains. Faced with those two little blue ticks of rejection, you can't help but jump to the worst conclusions. Was it something I said? Something I didn't say? Do they just hate me? *They must hate me.*

It's not just you. Researchers who have studied behaviour on messaging apps have found that a lot of us get antsy about read receipts. Around 2012, when the seen function was first introduced on Facebook Messenger, researchers at the University of Mannheim set out to see what people's expectations were around the feature. By surveying students, they found that people who felt a stronger need to belong and had a greater fear of ostracism felt more pressure to respond to 'seen' messages quickly, and expected their chat partners to respond quickly, too. People expected faster responses from chat partners they had a stronger relationship with, such as close friends, and also felt more obligation to respond quickly themselves when talking to these people.[1] 'The highest perceived obligation to answer, and the highest expectation for others, was romantic partners,' says Rainer Freudenthaler, one of the authors of the study, which leads us to another pro tip: never leave your partner on read.

Over time, however, Freudenthaler reckons that people have got a bit more used to read receipts. He insists that it doesn't make much difference to him these days. 'Most people I know don't really care if I answer late,' he says. That's what he thinks . . .

Given our general anxiety around being left on read, it's good etiquette to respond to messages as soon as you've read them. If you don't have time to give a full answer, send a quick message to say you'll respond properly later. On many apps (though not all), you can choose to turn read receipts off. The problem is that, when you disable them so that people can't see when you've read their messages, you also disable them so that *you* can't see when they have read *your* messages. And when you know that all it takes to see if someone's ignoring you or not is changing one little setting. . . well, if you're able to keep them turned off for any extended period of time, you are a stronger person than I am.

Alternatively, there is a workaround: if you read your messages on your phone's lock screen or notification panel without actually opening them, they don't show up as read to the sender. Sneaky.

Last seen

As well as the two little blue ticks of betrayal, you can usually surmise that someone is flagrantly ignoring your messages by when they were 'last seen' or 'active'. This displays the time someone last used the messaging app, so you can tell if they're really still asleep or if they were happily chatting away to other (clearly more important) people just two minutes ago.

As with read receipts, you can usually turn your 'last seen' or 'active' function off – but then you also can't see it for other people. On WhatsApp, you can still see when someone is 'online' regardless, meaning you know they have WhatsApp open and are connected to the internet. Of course, they could just be busy with other things and genuinely not have seen that you're trying to get through. A likely story.

Is typing . . .

The second most distressing signifier in messaging, after read receipts, is the typing awareness indicator. This lets you know that someone is in the process of drafting a response.

Sometimes, it looks like a little messaging bubble with an ellipsis in it. Sometimes, it pops up as 'So-and-so is typing'.

The typing awareness indicator can be very useful; if you see someone else is writing a message, you know to wait and let them finish before you interrupt. The problem is that, as with read receipts, we tend to read way too much into it. This is a situation in which silence really does speak much louder than words: if you see someone typing for ages, you expect a long message. If all you get at the end is 'OK', or even no message at all, you can't help but assume some kind of ulterior meaning. What did they *really* want to say?

Putting too much stock in the typing awareness indicator can also lead to the kind of farcical situation where one person notices the other is typing and so stops to let them go first, only for the other to notice they were also typing and so stop to let them go first, and so on – like when you get to a door at the same time as someone else and you both insist, 'After you,' 'No no, after you,' until you're stuck in an interminable dance of politeness.

THE FIVE STAGES OF GRIEF AFTER BEING LEFT ON READ

Denial: Great, they've seen my message! I'm sure they'll respond any moment now. Any moment now. . .

Anger: Bit rude, really.

Bargaining: Did I say something wrong?

Depression: I guess they must just hate me.

Acceptance: They are dead to me.

Try to have an idea of what you're going to say before you start tapping, so you don't end up in 'typing . . .' purgatory. Remember, messaging is meant to be informal and conversational; if you're writing something that requires extensive editing, it's probably time to put down the phone.

THE GROUP CHAT

MOST MESSAGING APPS have a group chat function, so that you can have a conversation with multiple people at the same time. Friendship circles today are defined by the group chat: if you're not in the chat, you're not in the crew.

The group chat as we know it is a relatively new phenomenon. Although chat rooms existed aeons ago in internet terms, people generally used these to speak to strangers, not people they knew in real life. When I recently asked my friends from university how we used to communicate and organise group activities before we had a shared WhatsApp group, we struggled to remember. Did we really just text people individually? Did we knock on people's doors unannounced? Did we. . . talk?

The thing is, it was simply impossible to have a sensible group discussion in a digital forum before people had smartphones. You'd have to get to your computer, check all the messages that had come since you last logged in, add your two cents, then wait for everyone else to get back to their computers to add their opinion. A ten-minute conversation could take days.

Now, it's easy. Select a few contacts, come up with a witty name for whatever assortment of people you're bringing together, and *bam*! You're in yet another chat group.

There are generally three types of messaging groups: long-term groups for defined circles of friends, intermittent groups for people with shared interests, and short-term groups created for specific events. Looking through my WhatsApp right now, I'm currently in a staggering 79 group chats – although the vast majority of these are inactive. At the top are the ones I regularly interact with, consisting of various groups of close friends and family members. Then there are the hobby groups, used to organise semi-regular meet-ups: the book club group, the *Mario Kart* group, the two different pub quiz groups (sorry teams, I'm cheating on you). Then there's a long list of groups dedicated to events gone by – festivals, weddings, New Year's Eve parties. Several are simply called 'Dinner'.

Group rules

Before you create a new group, make sure you're not already in one that serves the same function. Things get confusing when you have seven different permutations of the same group of friends, and this can easily lead to crossed wires and misunderstandings. Everyone's experienced that mortifying brain lapse where you accidentally send a message to the person you're talking *about* instead of *to* – imagine doing that, but with a load of mutual friends also in the group to bear witness to your shame.

If you're confident a new group is required, follow a few simple guidelines:

Be clear about what the group is for

Is this a general gossip group, or is it mainly functional? Choose a group name that communicates this, such as 'Knitting Club

Chit-Chat' or 'Knitting Club Meet-Up Admin'. People will be automatically notified when you add them to a group, but it's good form to send an initial message to explain why you're bringing people together.

Keep the group concise

Group chats are like email chains, in that the more people you add, the more unwieldy the message thread is likely to get. Adding too many people also makes a group feel less personal; a group chat of five close friends is much more intimate than a group chat of 15 people. Bear in mind also that when you add people into a group, their phone number will be visible to other group members, even if they don't know them, so this carries a certain level of responsibility.

Facebook Messenger allows you to have 250 people in a group and WhatsApp 256, but the thought that anyone could have any kind of meaningful conversation with that many people at once seems preposterous. Keep it to a maximum of around 10 people for a discussion-style group, or 20 for an event group. If you need to add many more, consider a less immediate form of communication that won't bombard everyone with notifications, such as a Facebook Event or a mass email (just make sure to follow the rules of CC).

Don't leave people out

Although you want to keep group numbers limited, people's feelings come first. No one likes to think they're being excluded from the gang, or that everyone else is talking behind their back. If you're making a group for everyone from knitting club, you do need to add *everyone* from knitting club, even if you all not-so-secretly think one person's really annoying.

Introduce newcomers

If you're adding people who don't know each other into the same group, make a brief introduction, just as if you were playing host at a real-life meeting. This is particularly important if you are adding new people to an existing group, as new members will not be able to see any messages that were sent before they joined. Make a simple announcement to bring everyone up to speed, like, 'Everyone, I've added Jan to the group – Jan, we were just talking about Jenny's bobble hat pattern.'

The one group that I strongly maintain you *don't* need is a work group. A group for friends from work? Sure. But leave the office chat to messengers designed specifically for business. Just think of it this way: in a group chat, you can only ever reply-all. (That, and it's probably a good rule to never hold work conversations on the same platform you use to send nudes.)

ALL THE GROUP CHATS YOU'RE PROBABLY IN

The family group

Your mum's discovered WhatsApp and adds you and your siblings to a group (she adds your dad too, but he never posts and you're not sure he even knows what it is). Safe topics of conversation include: holidays, what you're eating for dinner, and *The Great British Bake Off*. Things get more tense when the subject turns to as-yet-nonexistent grandchildren, career prospects, and *isn't Pamela from next door's newly single son just* lovely?

You and your siblings soon start a second group – without your parents.

Mum: A few photos from the first day of our cruise!!

Mum: [photo1]

Mum: [photo2]

Mum: [photo3]

Mum: [photo4]

Brother: Mum you know you can send more than one photo at once?

Mum: Oh! How do I do that?

Brother: Press the button with the plus sign on it when you go to add a photo

Mum: Like this?

Mum: [photo5]

Mum: [photo6]

Mum: [photo7]

Brother: No when you go to add a photo, press the plus sign

Mum: Do you mean a button on my phone?

Brother: No in the app

Mum: Do I need to download something?

Brother: Never mind

Mum: [photo8]

Mum: [photo9]

The passive-aggressive flatshare group

You've just moved in with your mates and you're psyched. What could be better than living full-time with your besties? You start the flatshare chat group full of enthusiasm, and name it after an in-joke that only you guys will understand. It starts out cute: you let each other know when you're going to be out, talk about a housewarming party that never actually happens, and ask if anyone wants anything from Tesco while you're passing.

As the shine wears off, things start to change. The group tone gets chillier; messages are now mainly for function, not fun. Conversations almost always devolve into debates over the cleaning rota, with attempts to use emoji to soften your requests failing to hide the obvious passive aggression.

You start quietly saving up to move into your own place.

Flatmate 1: Hey guys, don't want to be *that flatmate* but whose turn is it to clean the bathroom? It's looking pretty gross :)

*

Flatmate 2: Who used the last of the milk without replacing it? Remember we agreed milk is a shared good, I don't mind doing it this time but next time please replace it if you finish it ;)

*

Flatmate 3: Hi! Just to say can we stick to our agreed shower times please? Was nearly late for work <3

The neighbourhood watch group

This is like a flatshare group, except it includes everyone in your building or perhaps the whole street. What could possibly go wrong? You now know everything about your neighbours' lives, even if you wouldn't recognise them in person. Mary wants to start a gardening club; Joelle is trying to sell an old wardrobe; Howard is looking for a good divorce lawyer. But where the group really comes into its own is as a digital summit for your friendly neighbourhood curtain-twitchers and busybodies, who soon infest it with their Nimbyism and casual racism.

> Neighbour 1: SUSPICIOUS MALE spotted outside!! See attached picture, I only got the back of his head though. About 6 foot, looks Asian. Could this be the person who damaged the communal flower pots three weeks ago?
>
> Neighbour 2: Maybe!!! Have you called the police?
>
> Neighbour 1: Yes I left a message.
>
> Neighbour 2: Nice. Hopefully this time they will actually do their job!!!
>
> *
>
> Neighbour 3: Hello, can you please not report my dinner guests to the police in the future?
>
> Neighbour 1: Calm down, Neighbour 3, let's keep the group civil.

The music festival group

You're going to a festival with a gang of mates and you make a group to organise car-shares and camping supplies, and share rumours on the line-up. Once you've got to the venue and pitched your tents, you split up to see different acts. Afterwards, you message the group chat to try to arrange to meet up again – forgetting that everyone else is trying to do the same thing, no one's got any signal, and each message takes about 20 minutes to get through. You spend the rest of the evening like this:

Group 1: Hey! Meet at the tents in 20 minutes?

*

Group 2: Sure

*

Group 1: Oh sorry we already left – we're at the dance stage, about level with the third speaker on the right, next to the guy dressed in a unicorn onesie

*

Group 2: Are you still there? Can't see you. . .

*

Group 1: We're back at the tents!

*

Group 2: We're at the tents. Where are you?

*

Group 1: We just left the tents. Anyone seen Susie? We've lost her

*

Susie: I'm at the tents! Where is everyone?

The birthday party group

This is the inevitable group you find yourself added to any time someone's trying to organise an event. The host sends out the initial invitation and the RSVPs start rolling in. A few days later, the host invites more people they forgot the first time round, and they have to re-send all of the details again. Repeat until the day of the event, at which point:

> Host: Hi everyone, looking forward to seeing you all later today. Reminder that the address is 25B – ring the doorbell when you arrive
>
> *
>
> Guest 1: Hey! Was it 25A or 25B?
>
> Host: 25B! Ring the bell when you get here
>
> *
>
> Guest 2: On our way! What's the address again?
>
> Host: 25B, ring the bell
>
> Guest 2: Thanks :)
>
> *
>
> Guest 3: Hey! Anyone know the house number? And should we just ring the bell?

Optional: The lads' group

Want the definition of toxic masculinity? Just take a look at a male-only group chat. Often pulled together around a stag do, the lads' group is where even your wokest male friends become decidedly un-PC, all in the name of the group's primary goal: banter.

Sexist memes, poor-taste jokes and calling everyone a see-you-next-Tuesday is par for the course. One lad thinks it's really funny to keep changing the name and icon of the group, always to something you'd be embarrassed to be caught looking at. Another just shares porn gifs, and no one wants to tell him to cut it out, for fear of looking less macho. The more progressive lads' chats have finally got past the phase of using 'gay' as an insult, but they're still coming to grips with the idea of transgender people.

Lad 1: Oioi lads guess what I did last night

Lad 2: What?

Lad 1: YOUR MUM

Lad 3: hahahaha classic

Lad 4: lol legend

Lad 5: [porn gif]

Lad 6: *changes the group name to 'MILF Appreciation Society'*

GROUP CHAT ETIQUETTE

NOW YOU'VE GOT your group on the go, and you're happily chatting away. Unlike email, messaging is supposed to be fun – if you're filled with dread when you get a notification, you're doing friendship wrong. When you find yourself in 79 different chats at the same time, however, it can get a little overwhelming, and some basic etiquette will help keep things under control.

As with other forms of digital communication, timing is a major consideration in messaging etiquette. Be mindful of people's schedules. While prompt replies are preferred, not everyone can keep tap-tapping on their phone throughout the working day, so try not to hold any major discussions or make group decisions when you know someone's unavailable. In a group chat, a message won't be marked as read until everyone has seen it. (For discreet work-hour gossiping, many messengers have a desktop version that you can conveniently hide behind a Word document when the boss walks past. . .)

Keep messages in a group chat relevant to everyone, otherwise you're just clogging up people's feeds – like the WhatsApp version of an unnecessary email CC. Start a separate group if you're talking about an issue that not everyone is interested in, or if you're planning an event that not everyone in the first group is attending. Don't have a private chat in the group chat; that's just rude.

Speaking of clogging people's feeds, you should aim to minimise notifications. Don't send six separate messages in a row when one longer one will do. Anyone who has their notifications turned on will wonder what's possessed their phone when it starts non-stop buzzing, only to find out that it's. . .

. . . just you

. . . writing one message

. . . a few words

. . . at a time.

A conversation requires more than one person, so try to keep the discussion balanced and make sure everyone has a chance to contribute. If you're sending a lot more messages than you're receiving, you may need to calm down a bit and give someone else a chance to speak. That said, no one likes a lurker; if you're in a group, you should contribute at least occasionally. You don't need to be a Chatty Cathy, but it's kind of spooky if you stay silent and then chime in after everyone's forgotten you're there.

On a related note, don't wait for everyone else to respond first, especially when it comes to group decision-making. There's nothing more annoying than everyone waiting to see what everyone else thinks before giving their own opinion. If you have something to say, spit it (politely) out.

And can we all please agree one rule: If you propose an event or meeting, you must also suggest a time and location. There's little more irritating than when someone asks, 'Why don't we go for dinner this weekend?', receives a chorus of yeses, and then asks, 'Great, where?' This results in one of two things: radio silence, or a sudden influx of suggestions all across different parts of the city that happen to be convenient to the individual proposing them. The group becomes a standoff, with no one wanting to be the person who makes a decision. Take the initiative.

Finally, it is a law of messaging groups that what happens in the chat stays in the chat. Even if you're talking to a large group of people, you can assume that their messages are not meant for other people's eyes. Respect your friends' privacy, and don't share messages with others unless you have permission – even if you would get mad internet points if you put a screenshot on Twitter or Reddit. Resist the temptation to turn your friends into entertainment.

The art of the side chat

When you're talking to a group and sneakily have a separate private conversation with one or more friends within that group at the same time – a subgroup, if you will – you're engaging in a side chat. The ethics and etiquette here are rather fraught. Obviously, it's usually very rude to talk behind someone's back. That said, the side chat can be a godsend if you need to clarify something that's been said in the group, or just blow off steam to a close friend when things get too crazy.

Be warned, though: the side chat is not for amateurs. Having two chats on the go about the same topic at the same time is perilous territory when it comes to finger slips. Get the chats mixed up and you'll be sorry, as Labour MP Lucy Powell found out when she tried to send an angry message about some other MPs' positions on childcare to a couple of friendly colleagues. She instead accidentally sent it to a WhatsApp group that contained every female Labour MP – including those she was complaining about. It's more than likely that you too have experienced the sinking feeling when you've sent a message to the person you're talking about, rather than the intended recipient.

When this happens – and it is probably when, not if – then you have a race on to hit the 'delete' button before people see it. Not fast enough, and your only option is a swift and full *mea culpa*. In Powell's case, she soon noticed her error (although not soon enough) and apologised for 'being a cow'.[2]

See what I mean now about not having a work WhatsApp group?

As if the side chat weren't enough, I'm reliably informed that it's a common phenomenon to take screenshots of a conversation you're having with one annoying friend and share it with another in order to moan or laugh about it behind their back – like a side chat, but where the other person wasn't even in the chat to begin with. This is particularly duplicitous because people have a certain expectation of privacy when it comes to one-on-one messaging conversations, and would probably feel somewhat betrayed to learn you're secretly sharing their responses with someone else, much as you would if you heard your private conversation had been relayed to a third party.

It's pretty hard to justify this behaviour – really it's just pure bitchiness – so tread very carefully if you just can't resist. It's all too easy to accidentally screenshot a conversation and then send it back to the same friend – a dead giveaway you're maybe not being quite as sincere or trustworthy as you're trying to pretend.

Muting

If I had to choose one technology that has genuinely improved humanity's lot, it would have to be the mute function, which you can find across a range of platforms and which can be heaven sent when it comes to your message notifications. Just think of all the friendships it must have saved and the sanity it must have preserved, and there's probably a good case for whoever invented it to be handed a Nobel Peace Prize.

The mute setting in a messaging app turns off notifications for a conversation. You can still read all of the messages in the thread, but they won't make your phone buzz and they won't pop up on your screen one by one and distract you every three seconds. You can choose to turn off notifications for a set period of time, from hours to months, and other people in the group will not be alerted that you have muted the thread (although be warned: if you're messaging people in the group separately too, they will probably put two and two together).

Muting means you can still participate in a group chat without getting so distracted by it, so you can respond at your leisure. It comes in particularly handy if you get added to an overly large group, or one that involves hashing out details of an event: you can simply RSVP, then hit mute and sit back in peace as everyone squabbles over dates and directions. It's a way of bowing out of conversation without actually leaving, which can seem abrupt.

You need to be careful with muting a one-on-one conversation, as your lack of input is more likely to be noticed. There's a fine line between muting and just blatantly ignoring.

Leaving

When muting isn't enough, your only option is to leave the chat. If you leave, you won't be able to receive or send messages in the group any longer and will only be able to join again if you are re-invited by an admin. You should only do it, therefore, if you're absolutely certain you don't want to be in the group any more – for example, if it was created for an event that has now passed.

Never leave a group in anger, or to make a statement. When you exit, remaining group members will be notified, and that '. . . has left the group' message can look an awful lot like a petulant door-slam. You'll be sorry when you have to come grovelling to the group admin to let you back in.

For this reason, if you do need to leave a group, it's good manners to say goodbye first; just hitting 'exit' may be misinterpreted as an act of ghosting.

Blocking

If leaving a group chat is a last resort, then blocking is the nuclear option. If you block a contact, you will not receive any messages or calls from them. They will not be notified that you have blocked them, but they won't be able to see when you are online and won't see any updates to your profile. On WhatsApp, messages they send to you will appear with just one tick next to them, indicating that not only have they not been read, they've not even been delivered.

As blocking effectively eliminates contact, you should only use it if someone is really bothering you – like if they're a spammer, or your ex. If you block someone who you are also in a group chat with, you will still be able to see each other's messages in that group. It's pretty obvious that you've blocked someone if they can see you're active in a group chat but all their personal messages go undelivered.

QUIZ: MUTE, LEAVE, BLOCK

Forget *snog, marry, avoid*; when you're only looking to avoid, these are your options. In the following scenarios, select whether you should mute the chat, leave the group, or block the person. Answers below.

1. Your best friend added you to a group ahead of their stag or hen do, and their random school friends are still going strong with the photos, jokes and memes. It's getting tiresome, but your priority is not offending your bestie. Do you mute the chat, leave the group or block your friend?

2. You're in a family WhatsApp group and your mum has discovered a newfound love of emoji. The constant influx of messages is driving you crazy. Mute, leave or block?

3. Your ex-boyfriend or -girlfriend with whom you had a rather dramatic breakup got your new number off a mutual friend and wants to 'talk things over'. They've so far sent 12 messages and you haven't replied once.

4. You love your main group chat with all your mates, but you're having a rough day at work and need to focus. The constant messaging is getting distracting.

5. You're added to a huge group ahead of an event in order to arrange travel and logistics. You've RSVPed, sorted your transport and are all set to go, but there's still some time to go before the big day.

6. The big event is over, and everyone's back home safely. You're all still in the group, however. . .

7. You receive a message from someone you don't know. Their profile picture shows a voluptuous, scantily clad woman and they send you a flirtatious message with a link they ask you to click on to see more sexy pics.

8. The talk in your main friendship circle's group chat has turned to an upcoming event. You can't make it, however, and you're fed up of being reminded of what you're missing out on.

9. You're in a group with people who went to the same fitness class as you. But now you've moved away and joined a different class instead. You know you won't see them again.

10. A person you met on Tinder a while ago occasionally sends you suggestive messages out of the blue. You thought you'd made it clear you're not interested, but they won't take the hint and their messages make you uncomfortable.

Answers: *1. mute, 2. mute, 3. block, 4. mute, 5. mute, 6. leave, 7. block, 8. mute, 9. leave, 10. block.*

PHOTO AND VIDEO MESSAGES

G ONE ARE THE days when text messaging was limited to text; now, photos, videos and gifs allow for a smorgasbord of digital expression.

But just because it's an all-you-can-eat buffet doesn't mean you need to fill your plate. They say a picture is worth a thousand words, but a thousand pictures are just annoying. Be selective; send one or two photos rather than a whole reel. If you're sending multiple images, send them as one package rather than individually, so as not to clog the chat feed. Keep videos short, so that they don't take a long time to download or view. No one wants to watch your fuzzy gig videos.

Photos and videos shared in a message are more personal than those put on public social media channels. It's fine to share a few holiday snaps, but the best photo messages are those that make your friends feel like a real part of your life. Friends don't want to see your perfectly-posed Instagram beach bod, they want to see your candid ugly selfie.

On apps like Snapchat, messaging is done almost entirely through photos and videos. Here, reciprocity is the rule; if someone snaps you, you're expected to snap back. If you exchange snaps with a friend every day for three days or more, you'll start a 'Snapstreak', which means a fire emoji will appear next to your friend's name in your contacts list, with the number of days the streak has been going for counted down next to it. If you fail to snap each other over one 24-hour period, you will lose your streak and have to start again. Needless to say, friends don't let friends' Snapstreaks die.

Voice messages

Some messengers allow you to record short voice memos instead of typing a message. This feature can be very useful for people who find text messaging difficult, for example if you have poor eyesight or another condition that means you struggle to type on the phone keyboard. Some people also find voice memos more convenient if they're messaging while doing something and don't have their hands free. And some people just love to hear the sound of their own voice.

Used properly, voice memos can add that extra special something that a text message just can't capture. Used improperly, all they add is that extra special annoyance.

A voice message might be more convenient for you, but it probably isn't for your friends. As most of us read a lot faster than we speak, it almost always takes longer to listen to a voice memo than to glean the same information from a text message.

Keep them short – ideally under a minute. Messaging should be conversational, but voice memos soon become monologues. No one wants to have to pause their favourite podcast at a crucial moment just to listen to your 15-minute debrief about last night's Tinder date before they can rejoin the conversation. Never send multiple voice memos in a row. If your finger slips off the record button before you're finished, your message is too long.

If you have a good story to tell that just can't be adequately conveyed by text, set up a phone call or save it for a face-to-face conversation. You need to keep *something* for real life.

Phone calls

OK, let's get one thing clear: *do not call unannounced unless someone's dying.*

In fact, even then, send a text first.

Don't get me wrong, I'm all for phone calls. A voice call is much closer to a face-to-face chat than messaging and is therefore much more personal. You know the person on the other end is engaged right at that moment – there's no blue-ticking here – so it's perfect both if you want a snappy answer or a proper chat. A phone call also benefits from added tone of voice, which can still communicate emotion a lot better than even the most carefully selected emoji.

It's for these same reasons, however, that phone calls are much more inconvenient. You need to give the conversation your relatively undivided attention for the duration; you can't choose to respond later. Calling out of the blue can therefore put people out, especially if you plan to speak for more than a couple of minutes. Send a message first to check it's a good time. If it's not, arrange a time that is. If your call is urgent, send a message saying as much. This at least gives the other person a chance to clear any immediate obligations and mentally prepare themselves.

When you are on a call, make sure you're in the moment. That gentle tapping sound in the background is a clear indication that you're actually scrolling round the internet instead of properly listening. . .

Voicemails

There is literally no good reason to ever leave a voicemail, in a personal context as much as a work context.

Voicemails are the most annoying, time-wasting thing. You get the notification – *You have one. New. Message* – and then have to go through the rigmarole of dialing your answerphone, going through the robot-voice menu – *To listen to your messages, press 1* – and listening to the message before you even know what it's about. (Incidentally, you'll almost always assume it's bad news, which adds to the feeling of dread.) Then the message turns out to be a 30-second clip of your mother saying that she's *'just checking in, don't worry there's nothing important, just thought we hadn't had a chat in a while, don't feel you have to ring me back immediately, maybe we can talk one evening this week, hope you're well, I'm sure you're out somewhere having fun, OK, bye bye, talk soon, bye bye, call me back, bye.'*

End of messages. To listen to the message again, press 1...

If you try to call someone and can't get through, hang up and send a text message instead.

Video calls

Video calls, the kind you make through Skype or FaceTime, are the closest technological solution you can get to speaking to someone in person. Not only can they hear you, they can also see you, with all your facial expressions and gestures displayed in beautiful, glitchy technicolour. A video call is perfect for letting the grandparents chat to their grandkids, staying in touch with a friend from back home, or keeping a long-distance relationship aflame.

But it's also hard work. A video call demands full attention, even more so than a phone call, monopolising both your eyes and ears. It's therefore even more important to schedule a video call in advance. When you do so, make sure to specify that it will be a video call, so your conversation partner doesn't accidentally pick up when they're half-naked or picking their nose. If you haven't agreed on video, start with a voice call and then ask if they are happy to switch.

When you're on a video call, try to avoid the temptation of staring at your own face and keep your attention on the person you're talking to. Remember, you're not taking a selfie. Don't get too close to the camera; no one wants to find themselves talking to your nose hair. If the picture starts to lag or lose quality, you may want to switch to a voice call, as pixelated images and out-of-sync video are very distracting.

SHOULD YOU MAKE A PHONE CALL?

SHOULD YOU LEAVE A VOICEMAIL?

DECODING DIGITAL CONVERSATIONS

NOW WE'VE COVERED the essentials of good messaging behaviour, we're faced with the question of what – and how – to write. Messaging is an informal medium, so a conversational manner, slang vocabulary and the occasional autocomplete mistake are all perfectly accepted and expected. These are supposed to be your friends, after all.

That said, as with other forms of written communication, it can sometimes be difficult to get your true meaning across when you're limited to a keyboard and don't have the benefit of non-verbal cues such as facial expressions and tone of voice. How can you show when you're being sarcastic? Did your friend mean that comment as a joke or an insult? Is that 'OK' enthusiastic or begrudging?

Fear not, because thanks to the delightful flexibility of language and the creativity of human communication, we've come up with a whole range of creative ways to make sure our messages are correctly interpreted.

Emoji

One linguistic flourish that has come to define digital communication among friends is emoji. The smartphone's upgrade to emoticons – remember those? :-) – emoji offer a cute, informal way to convey a simple idea or to add a bit of extra emotional context to a message. Often, emoji are used as a shorthand for expressing sentiment. Want to show you're happy about something? Use the smiley emoji. Say congratulations? The clinking champagne glass.

Linda Kaye, a senior lecturer in psychology at Edge Hill University, says that emoji can be broadly split into two camps: facial emoji and object emoji. Facial emoji are the little smiles and frowns that convey facial expressions, and object emoji are all the others – the animals, flowers, food, flags and various train-like vehicles included just in case you really need to distinguish between a tram, trolley bus and light railway, plus those Japanese ones you're not quite sure about (half a potato? Some kind of biscuit?).

Facial emoji are the most commonly used. Kaye says that these are usually used to add an emotional element to written communication or to help reduce ambiguity around a message, such as signalling to a recipient that a message is meant sarcastically. 'It's something known as hypertextual communication – this idea that we've compensated for the lack of non-verbal cues by using emoji and other techniques,' she explains.

Kaye and her colleagues have studied how basic facial

emoji change people's understanding of a text. Their research on this is currently under review, but they provisionally found that when people were given the same text, they were significantly more likely to view it as more positive when it had a smiley emoji attached and negative when it had a frowny emoji. When an ambiguous emoji was attached – the face with eyes but no mouth – people were much less confident in their rating. These findings may sound rather obvious, but they show that emoji aren't just silly little doodles and can actually be a useful tool to make sure your message isn't taken the wrong way.

Emoji can also reveal something about the person using them. Looking at people's use of emoji on Facebook, Kaye and her colleagues found that people judged those who used happy emoji as more open, agreeable and conscientious. They also found that people who used a more diverse range of emoji, and not just the happy faces, were more open-minded.[3]

If speaking to someone you don't know well, you probably want to limit yourself to the most common emoji; not everyone is emoji-fluent, and once you get past the first screen in the emoji keyboard, they can get a little confusing. If people are struggling to tell the difference between a teardrop and a bead of sweat, they're probably not appreciating the full sense of your message (are you sad? Anxious? Just been jogging?).

Kaye says she most commonly uses the 'face with tears of joy' emoji – which Apple said in 2017 was the most frequently used emoji on its platforms[4] – and the winking face, which she uses to indicate sarcasm. 'A lot of it is to do with the person and what kind of impression you want to give of yourself,' she says. 'I'm quite cheeky sometimes, so I quite like to just put them on to show a bit about me.'

A note on emoji skin tone

In 2015, the Unicode Consortium – the body that approves new emoji, as well as overseeing other character standards – introduced more racial diversity into the standard emoji set. The default emoji colour remains bright yellow (which is intended as a non-human shade), but users can now also choose from five different skin tones.

Most people choose either the default yellow or the emoji they feel best represents them. If you are white, however, it's best to always stick to yellow. Using the lightest skin tone can come off as a bit, well, *white power*, while using a brown or black emoji when it doesn't reflect your real-world identity is controversial: some suggest it can be interpreted as an expression of solidarity, but others argue that it's tantamount to digital blackface. Of course, using the 'default' shade as white is problematic in itself, but for now it's the best of a bunch of imperfect options.

Object emoji

Philip Seargeant, a lecturer in applied linguistics at the Open University, says that people use object emoji differently to facial emoji, and often in very creative, idiosyncratic ways. Different communities adopt emoji in different ways and imbue them with new significance. His friends, for example, have a WhatsApp group where they discuss politics. Whenever someone agrees with a point, they send an owl emoji – their own version of a 'like' button. 'I'm not quite sure why, but that's what they do,' he says. These little quirks and in-jokes are the glue that hold friendship groups together.

Some emoji have also taken on more general second meanings. Beyond the euphemistic emoji covered in Chapter 2, several other characters have taken on special significance in everyday conversation. The nail polish emoji, for instance, expresses a sense of girl-power-style accomplishment, while the woman with one hand raised (officially supposed to represent an 'information desk person') indicates a sassy attitude. The upside-down face is often used to show sarcasm.

Be aware, however, that not all emoji appear identically across platforms. Different operating systems and apps can offer slightly different versions of the same emoji, which means things occasionally get lost in translation. The Apple dancer emoji might look like a fierce party girl, but her Samsung sister has more of a dad-dancing vibe.

The Emojipedia website is a good resource for looking up what an emoji means and how it appears across all different platforms. Meanwhile, if you're dealing with a situation that requires particular care or nuance, you're probably best sticking to good old-fashioned words. In 2016, pop legend Cher had to publicly apologise after tweeting in support of victims of a terror attack in Turkey – using a bomb emoji. She acknowledged that the emoji was 'poorly placed' and 'insensitively timed'. Quite.

Emoticons

While emoji have largely superseded emoticons, the old-school smileys still have their charms :) Japanese emoticons, or *kaomoji*, can be particularly expressive; somehow emoji can't quite communicate the depth of sentiment captured in my personal favourites, the shruggie: ¯_(ツ)_/¯ and the table flip: (╯°□°)╯︵ ┻━┻

Given these borrow Japanese characters, they're pretty cumbersome to type; your best bet is to just google, copy and paste. Or if you're a habitual shrugger, you can of course set up a shortcut to type it with ease.

Gifs

Gifs (pronounced with a hard 'g', thank you) are animated images that last just a couple of seconds long. They can consist of cartoons or snippets of films, TV shows, or other videos. You can find huge repositories of gifs on sites such as Giphy.com, and many messaging apps have a gif search function directly in the app, which lets you type in a word and find related gifs. In WhatsApp, this is located next to the emoji keyboard.

In the context of messaging, the most common type of gif is a 'reaction gif'. These are gifs that portray an emotional response to something that has been said – like the emoji's bigger, animated cousin. They usually consist of a film or TV character's facial expression. Fed up? Try an over-the-top eye roll courtesy of actress Krysten Ritter in the TV show *Don't Trust the B---- in Apartment 23*. Confused? Winona Ryder's puzzled expression at the Screen Actors Guild Awards has you covered. Shocked? One of my favourites is a gif of a snowy owl with its beak opening, slowly turning its head as if in disbelief.

You can also make your own gifs using online tools such as Giphy Gif Maker or Imgur's Video to Gif tool. These sites let you drop in the URL of a YouTube video or upload your own video file and select a few seconds to turn into a gif that you can then drop into your chat or on social media as a bespoke touch.

How to laugh online

It seems to be a rule that emotions must be exaggerated in text. You can't simply laugh at something, you must laugh out loud, or roll on the floor laughing. You must laugh so hard you're crying, even if in reality your facial muscles haven't so much as twitched.

Although 'LOL' is still in regular usage, it's much less common than other forms of digital laughter these days. According to a Facebook report in 2015, laughing emoji like the 'tears of joy' face featured in around a third of people's attempts at communicating laughter, while 'LOL' made up only 2 per cent. The most common form of laughter, however, was variations on 'haha', which made up just over half of total laughs analysed. The remaining 13 per cent of digital laughs were by those creeps who say 'hehe' instead.[5]

GRAMMAR AND PUNCTUATION

EMOJI AND GIFS aren't the only way of adding a shot of emotion or a dash of tone to a message. When it comes to text-based communications, we've become incredibly resourceful at finding ways to show what we really mean using just the characters and grammar already available to us.

Messaging is fast and casual, so it's quite normal to be pretty lax about grammar and punctuation. In fact, a message that uses 'proper' grammar, with punctuation marks, capitalisation and so on, risks looking cold or officious. You're supposed to be chatting to your mates here, not delivering a lecture; insist on using semi-colons in all of your WhatsApp chats and you'll probably come across as the kind of irritating smartarse who comments on strangers' social media posts just to correct their language.

Full stops

Only old people or troubled souls put full stops at the end of every message. It's true: in 2016, even the *New York Times* reported that the once-imperative punctuation mark was dying, or at least 'going out of style'. The piece quoted eminent British linguist David Crystal as saying that, 'We are at a momentous moment in the history of the full stop' – all because of instant messaging.

The thing is, in a messaging conversation, a full stop is simply not necessary. It's clear when you've finished your thought already, so what function does the full stop fulfil? As a result, using a full stop in messaging now looks rather emphatic, and can come across as if you're quite cross or annoyed. There's something so final about it. 'It looks as if you're making a point,' Seargeant observes.

Consider this perfectly normal response from a perfectly normal person:

- So I'll see you later?
- OK

Now compare to this spine-chilling exchange with a probable axe-murderer:

- So I'll see you later?
- OK.

OK. OK. . . what? Did I do something wrong? Are you mad at me?

While full stops at the end of sentences might be on a downwards slope, they can find themselves redistributed elsewhere, where they can be placed very deliberately in order to add emphasis. Take, for example, the trend of wedging one between every word for dramatic effect. Just. Look. How. Emphatic. This. Is.

Capital letters

It's not unusual to drop capitalisation at the beginning of a sentence in messaging, even going so far as to use the lower-case first-person pronoun 'i'. Sometimes, this is down to speed; sometimes, it's a deliberate choice to emphasise the informal or lighthearted nature of a message.

Writing in all-caps, meanwhile, is generally understood to mean that YOU ARE SHOUTING.

Capitalising the first letter of words or phrases that aren't normally capitalised in English can be used for ironic effect, to sarcastically suggest that something is a Matter of Great Importance, or to draw attention to a Tiresome Stereotype or Trope (see: the Nice Guy).

Question marks

The question mark is another victim of messaging laziness. Like the full stop, it's simply not needed a lot of the time. It's often obvious when a question is a question, and so the mark becomes redundant.

– Hey, how are you

gets the point across just as effectively as:

– Hey, how are you?

Sometimes, people deliberately leave question marks off in order to indicate that a question is rhetorical, sarcastic, or intended in a deadpan tone. See:

– What is actually wrong with you?

which sounds really rather accusatory, versus:

132

– what is actually wrong with you

in which you can almost see the speaker knowingly smiling and shaking their head.

Exclamation marks

British fantasy author Terry Pratchett held that using multiple exclamation marks in a row was a sign of certain insanity, proclaiming through one of his characters in his Discworld novel *Maskerade* that using five exclamation marks was 'a sure sign of someone who wears his underpants on his head'. He clearly wasn't in a WhatsApp group with any of my friends.

Unlike the full stop and question mark, the exclamation mark runs no risk of dying out; on the contrary, it has become perfectly normal to use many more than the standard single one. As a general rule, the more exclamation marks you use, the more excited you are!!! (Although to be fair to Pratchett, more than five does start getting a bit ridiculous!!!!)

An exclamation mark can even be a complete sentence. It suggests a reaction of shock or excitement, acting as a shorthand for 'Wow!' or 'What?!' or 'How exciting!'

– I got the job!

– !

– !!!

Ellipses

Ellipses – indicating a pause. . . uncertainty. . . or that there's more to come. . . – are used more frequently in messaging than in formal writing. You can use an ellipsis in place of a spoken pause or slow voice, to suggest a dramatic pause or hesitation. It's not uncommon to shorten the three-dot ellipsis to two dots.

Used at the end of a message, an ellipsis either means the person hasn't finished and there's more to come (look to the typing indicator for a clue), that they are trailing off into deep thought, or that they would like some input from their conversation partner.

Grammar traditionalists, look away now, but you might even witness some people using the nascent 'comma-ellipsis' – an ellipsis made of two or three commas instead of full stops. This is by no means widely used, and only ever in a very informal context , , ,

The nuances of the comma ellipsis have not yet been codified, but a call-out to my Twitter followers garnered several potential explanations, with some people suggesting that it indicates irony or is meant as a less 'serious' version of the regular ellipsis, which to some people apparently looks a bit angry these days. . .

Or, of course, it might just indicate that someone's finger slipped on the keyboard.

Text formatting

In some messaging apps, you can use the following codes to format text for extra emphasis:

text – bold
text – italic
~text~ – strikethrough

On platforms that don't automatically change these marks into formatting, they can be placed around words to give them a different meaning. A pair of asterisks around a word can indicate emphasis, but is also sometimes used to describe an action, like a sort of digital stage direction.

- Finally got home from work *sigh*

Used sparingly, these can be fun, but things get a bit weird when you start role-playing whole scenes. Leave that to the odd guys trying to act out their fantasies over Tinder *tips fedora*.

You can use a sole asterisk to indicate a correction to a preceding statement, as in:

- The party starts at 6pm

- *7pm

A pair of tildes around a word generally suggests that something is ~quirky~. This can also be used in a ~mocking~ way, like a punctuation eye-roll. Tildes combined with asterisks, sometimes referred to as ~*~sparkly unicorn punctuation~*~, was a trademark of teenage girls and emo kids back in the early noughties.

There are a couple of other formatting tricks you can use to add a bit of emotional oomph to your words too, such as s p a c i n g t h e m o u t to show that you're speaking s l o w l y or being very d e l i b e r a t e with your word choice. You can also add exxxxxtra letters for emphasis, or to suggest a kind of draaaawl.

The secret vocabularies of friendship groups

Fifteen years ago, Philip Seargeant says, people used to talk about 'netspeak' or 'internet English' as if it were a distinct dialect. But it's impossible to draw such a clear set of rules, as each online community tends to have its own linguistic quirks and adopt its own slang and jargon. 'We've got to the point where there are so many different types of online platforms that just talking about "online" as a thing is no longer really helpful,' he says.

Often, one community's slang can appear completely unintelligible to outsiders. Take parenting site Mumsnet, which has its own dictionary of acronyms. Here, a member's family is referred to by terms like DH, DW, DS and DD – meaning 'darling/dear husband', 'darling/dear wife', 'darling/dear son', 'darling/dear daughter', and so on. Not everyone gets the 'darling/dear' treatment – you'll quite often see a MIL (mother-in-law) or FIL (father-in-law) without the D prefix, and then there's the STBXH ('soon-to-be-ex-husband').

Things get particularly tricky when different communities use the same terms to mean completely different things. On Mumsnet, BC does not refer to two thousand years ago, but to the era 'before children'. And a boyfriend isn't a BF, as on many other forums – that acronym is reserved for 'breastfeeding'. Instead, they're a DP – which stands for 'darling/dear partner', but which, in seedier corners of the internet, means something rather more NSFW.

Common acronyms

There is, however, some digital vocabulary that has become widely adopted across different groups. While text speak, sometimes known rather gloriously as 'disemvowelling', has generally gone out of fashion, some of the acronyms it ushered in have fared better. Many are no longer common – remember when 'LOL' meant 'lots of love' instead of 'laughing out loud'? – but others have stuck around. It's increasingly common to see them written in lowercase rather than all-caps.

20 COMMON ACRONYMS

AFAIK – as far as I know

BTW – by the way

FTW – for the win

FWIW – for what it's worth

FYI – for your information

ICYMI – in case you missed it

IDK – I don't know

IIRC – if I recall correctly

IKR – I know, right?

IMO/IMHO - in my (humble) opinion

IRL – in real life

JK – just kidding

LOL – laugh out loud

LMK – let me know

NP – no problem

OMG – oh my god

SMH – shaking my head (in disbelief/disapproval)

TBF – to be fair

TBH – to be honest

WTF/WTAF – what the (actual) fuck (also WTH – what the hell)

SMARTPHONE ETIQUETTE

INALLY, WHEN IT comes to friendship, it's important to make sure digital communication isn't overshadowing your real-world interactions. Debrett's states firmly that 'answering phone calls, texting, or even repeatedly glancing at the screen in a social situation is never acceptable', but this seems a little estranged from the realities of modern life. It's certainly true that you should always prioritise living, breathing company over the people in your phone, but light smartphone usage is these days generally accepted in casual social environments.

Still, you should keep distraction to a minimum. It's fine to send the occasional message or take the odd photo, but it's not OK to spend 15 minutes gawping at Twitter while others

---

SMARTPHONE BODY
LANGUAGE DECODER

Glancing repeatedly at phone – *I'm busy, can we wrap this up?*

Absent-mindedly scrolling through social media – *I'm bored.*

Staring fastidiously at screen and not looking up – *Don't talk to me.*

Wearing headphones – *Do. Not. Talk. To. Me.*

---

chat around you. Play it by ear; if you're the only one with your phone out, put it away. You should at least avoid using smartphones at the dinner table (after you've Instagrammed your meal, of course).

The rules are a bit stricter if you're having a one-on-one conversation with someone, as in this case being on your phone means you're definitely ignoring a real-life friend, which is rude regardless. This is sometimes rather clumsily referred to as 'phubbing' – snubbing someone in favour of your phone. Think of it like leaving someone on read, except they can see with their own eyes that you're texting someone else instead.

Looking repeatedly at your phone has replaced glancing at your watch as the universal sign of 'I'm bored or busy or just really want to be somewhere else.' If you notice a friend doing this, it may be your cue to slurp down the rest of your coffee and wrap things up.

MEMES, MANSPLAINERS AND MILKSHAKE DUCKS

THE ART OF COMMUNITY

FIVE GOLDEN RULES

1. No mansplaining

2. No vaguebooking

3. No humblebragging

4. No tweetstorming

5. No pictures of avocado on toast

As if communicating privately weren't enough of an etiquette challenge, social media lets us all share our deepest thoughts, dankest memes and fleekest selfies with just about anyone – friends, followers, strangers, and that weird kid from high school who still likes all your Facebook posts.

Online communities date back to the beginning of the internet. It started with things like Usenet and bulletin boards, which worked in a similar way to what we now call online forums. The first social networking sites launched in the 1990s; readers who had their formative online experiences when the internet was still dial-up may recall looking up old school friends on Classmates or pouring out their teen angst in diary entries on LiveJournal.

Then came the noughties, and the rise of many of today's biggest social media sites. LinkedIn was founded in May 2003, Facebook in 2004 and Twitter in 2006. For each platform that has stayed the course, others have gone out of fashion – RIP Friendster, Myspace and Bebo. The 2010s saw a rise in more image-focused sites and apps, including Instagram, Pinterest and Snapchat. (2011 also saw the launch of Google+, but people cared about that as much then as they do now.)

Every social media site is different. They offer different features, appeal to different audiences and have different expectations when it comes to behaviour. What is perfectly acceptable in one community may be unthinkable in another.

We also use each platform differently; research looking at people's profile pictures and written bios across platforms shows that we present different 'personas' on each one.[1]

Go to my LinkedIn and you'll get the impression that I'm an accomplished professional. Follow me on Twitter and you'll be blown away by my searing wit. Scroll through my Instagram and you'll realise that, actually, I'm just a crazy cat lady.

All of this makes social media a digital etiquette minefield. What's the difference between a friend and a 'friend'? What are RTs if not endorsements? And what would Debrett's have to say about memes? The stakes are high: play things right, and you could be propelled to online celebrity. Play them wrong, and you could be condemned to infamy. Just ask Milkshake Duck.

GETTING SET UP

YOUR PROFILE ON different social media platforms should reflect whichever side of you you wish to present in that milieu. Some, such as Facebook and LinkedIn, aim to reflect real-world relationships, and as such require or at least strongly encourage you to use your real name. Others take the opposite approach: anonymity is common on many forums and discussion groups, with most people choosing to go by a pseudonym. The good thing about anonymity is that it helps people feel free to express their real opinions. The bad thing about anonymity is that it helps people feel free to express their real opinions.

Twitter and Instagram fall somewhere in the middle, with

WHAT YOUR TWITTER BIO SAYS ABOUT YOU

'Coffee' as an interest – *You're basic.*

Coffee-themed joke – *Still basic.*

A long list of interests and hobbies – *You think you're on Tinder.*

Every place you've ever worked – *You think you're on LinkedIn.*

'Guru', 'ninja', 'rockstar' – *You need to get a real job.*

'Addict', 'junkie', 'aficionado' – *You've confused having a hobby with having a personality.*

A list of cities next to the plane emoji – *You've confused having money with having a personality.*

'Mummy to'/'Daddy to' – *You're on here before most people have woken up. You have strong views on breastfeeding.*

'Gamer' – *You're a misogynist.*

'Patriot' (not the sports team) – *You're a racist.*

'Jedi' – *You work in IT.*

A meaningful quote – *You're either a 13-year-old girl or a business 'evangelist' (it's often surprisingly hard to tell the difference).*

A link to your Soundcloud – *You still haven't given up your dreams of being a rapper.*

No bio – *You're either a nobody, or you're Beyoncé.*

'Views my own' – *Don't worry hun, you really aren't as important as you think you are.*

some people opting to use their real names and others choosing to go by a nickname. Which you choose depends on the persona you want to portray. Are you posting as yourself? Your business? Or your comedy alter-ego, TheChucklingCupcake?

Like dating sites, many social media sites these days forgo an in-depth written profile, although it's a good idea to add a short bio on platforms such as Twitter and Instagram to let prospective followers know a bit about you. You should aim for people to be able to quickly skim your profile and immediately get an idea of who you are (or who you'd like them to think you are). You can include details such as your job title, location and interests, but try to avoid getting too overtly self-promotional, which is just tacky. It's fine to add a link to your website/blog/newsletter/YouTube, but limit yourself to one at a time.

When it comes to profile pictures, bear in mind that any image you upload to the internet may stick around for quite some time. When I recently searched for my own name on Google Images (don't judge), the top results included a picture I once uploaded to Twitter that now makes me recoil from my screen with embarrassment. In it, I am wearing Google Glass.

FRIENDS AND FOLLOWERS

YOUR EXPERIENCE ON social media will largely be shaped by the people you connect with, so choose wisely. There are two main types of connection across platforms: friends and followers. Friendship is mutual; you can only be friends with someone if they also want to be friends with you. Following, however, is often one-sided. You'll never be Beyoncé's *friend* (sorry), but there's no excuse not to be her *follower*.

Facebook friends

In theory, your Facebook friends should be your real-life friends. In practice, you're probably not as popular as your Facebook friend list suggests.

Facebook lets you connect with up to 5,000 people, but Robin Dunbar, a professor of evolutionary psychology at the University of Oxford, says the number of actual friends we can have is closer to 150. Dunbar came up with this number – now known appropriately as 'Dunbar's number' – 25 years ago, after observing a correlation between the size of primates' brains and the size of their social groups, which he then extrapolated to human brain size. Essentially, he argues that we don't have the time or brain power to keep more than around 150 real friend-ships on the go at any one time – and he doesn't think the internet has changed that.[2]

Dunbar defines a friend as someone with whom you have a meaningful relationship and regular contact (this includes family members). He describes it to me as people who would willingly do you a favour without asking for anything in return, and who would expect the same from you. 'They won't argue about being paid back; they'll just assume you will,' he says. Although he puts the average number of friends at 150, he says the figure can vary from 100 to 250; younger people and people with more extraverted personalities are likely to be towards the higher end of the spectrum.

Past that point, however, and your 'friends' aren't really *friends*; they're more likely to be acquaintances. They could be friends of friends, people you work with or, as in my case, all the people you met in Freshers' Week at university and haven't spoken to since.

Dunbar reckons that many people include some of this acquaintance layer into their Facebook friend list. 'A few people click "yes" every time they're asked if they want to befriend somebody,' he says. 'Really, all they're doing is doing what we do in everyday life, which is bringing the acquaintance layer into the digital format.' He puts the number of acquaintances a person can have at around 500 – strikingly close to my own Facebook friend count.

Who you decide to friend really depends on how intimate you want to keep your digital social circle. You should at least *know* people you try to connect with – friend requests from strangers are just creepy. If you want to keep your circle small, it's perfectly fine to politely decline a request (although good luck explaining that to your mother). If someone declines your friend request, accept it with good grace and do not re-send the request.

FACEBOOK FRIEND BINGO

How many of these appear in your Facebook friends list?

- Your first crush
- At least one former teacher
- That scrawny kid from school who's now a bodybuilder
- That scrawny kid from school who's now a glamour model
- A one-night stand
- Someone you met at a festival and were convinced you'd be best friends with but haven't seen or spoken to a single time since
- The creepy guy from work
- An extended family member you can't quite remember how you're related to
- Your mum

- Your mum's friend
- Someone you don't recognise because they've changed their name
- Someone you don't recognise because they've had plastic surgery
- Someone you just don't recognise (who actually are they?)
- A deactivated account
- Your kid niece/nephew (just joking – they're not on here, Facebook is for old people)

Unfriending

Choosing to break off a social media friendship is much more meaningful than just not connecting with someone in the first place. It's a clear snub. You *did* think they were worth connecting with, but now you don't.

If you haven't had contact with someone for a while, you may get away with unfriending them without them noticing, but it's always a risk. In cases where you need to be a little more tactful, there's another option. Similar to muting someone on messaging apps, you can 'unfollow' a person's account on Facebook, which means that while they remain your friend in principal, you will no longer see their posts in your newsfeed. It's the diplomatic way to ignore someone.

If you do decide to do a bit of a friend spring-clean, just go about it quietly. Posting one of those obnoxious 'Just did a friend cull so congrats if you're reading this, you made the cut' statuses is the height of poor taste.

Twitter and Instagram followers

Unlike friending, following someone isn't necessarily an indication that you know or even like them – hence Piers Morgan's 6.4 million Twitter followers. Instead, you should follow anyone whose output you find interesting (even if it's just because you want to argue with it). Follow your friends. Follow people in your industry. Follow people you find funny, interesting or intelligent. Follow parody dog accounts. Check your following list – is it mainly white men? Find some women, non-binary folk and people of colour you admire and follow them too.

Don't get too follow-happy, though. Twitter lets you follow 5,000 accounts before it starts to restrict following numbers, but if you don't put some effort into curating who you follow, your feed will soon become unmanageable and you'll miss the updates you actually want to see.

There are two main approaches when it comes to Twitter and Instagram. Some people use these platforms in a personal capacity, connecting mainly with people they already know IRL. Others take great pride in amassing as many followers as possible, with dreams of becoming an #influencer.

Some do both, creating two accounts for different purposes: one for their public persona and one that they keep private and share only with actual friends. On Instagram, this second account is sometimes referred to as a 'finsta' (a portmanteau of 'fake' and 'Instagram') and is used to share more personal, unfiltered shots with select followers, compared to the highly curated life presented on a user's real ('rinsta') account.

The following:follower ratio

As a rule, having more people follow you than you are following is an indication that you're doing something right. Try not to let your ego get too hung up on it, though. A high follower count alone isn't a mark of quality (see again: Piers Morgan), and the worst social media etiquette faux pas you can make is trying to increase your popularity through artificial means.

One common and slightly sleazy trick is to follow lots of people in the hope that they'll follow back. Or worse: follow lots of people in the hope that they'll follow back, then unfollow them when they haven't responded, then follow them *again* in the hope that maybe *this time* they'll follow back. While you might get away with it sometimes, it's only a matter of time before someone calls you out. Some desperate souls don't even try to hide their motivations, blatantly tagging pleas like #followforfollow or #followback.

Avoid this approach; we can all see what you're doing. The only real way to get more followers is to engage with the community (or you can just buy fake followers from dodgy corners of the internet – but it's kind of obvious when your count suddenly jumps by a nice round number).

How your following:follower ratio stacks up

1:1 million+	You are Beyoncé-level famous
1:100,000	You are very famous
1:10,000	Still famous
1:1,000	You'd count as a celebrity of some kind
1:100	You're an #influencer
1:10	You're quite good at this
1:1	You're a normal person
10:1	You're still a normal person
100:1	Not many of your friends are on here, are they?
1,000:1	:(

Verified accounts

Many social media sites offer a 'verified badge' to show that someone's account is authentic. On Twitter and Instagram, this is the coveted blue tick that appears next to people's names. The exact criteria for getting one are kept pretty murky. They're generally reserved for public figures, so that users can tell that politicians, celebrities and so on really are who they say they are and not an impostor.

Who exactly counts as a public figure, however, appears to be relatively arbitrary. A verified badge really doesn't confer much more to the beholder than a sense of smugness, and there's no need to get in a tizzy over it. Certainly don't do what WikiLeaks editor Julian Assange did when Twitter refused to verify his account and put the blue diamond emoji next to your name to try to fool people into thinking you have a blue tick. Tragic.

Likes and favourites

The minimal form of interaction you can have on most social media sites (other than lurking, of course) is 'liking' or 'favouriting'. The iconic example is Facebook's Like button, the little blue 'thumbs-up' sign. Twitter and Instagram, meanwhile, both have little red hearts.

A like can mean much more than just 'I like this'. It can say 'I agree with you,' or 'I think you look fit,' or 'I'm sorry your dog died'. Context is crucial, so if there's any ambiguity over why you're liking your friend's post about their cat's funeral, be sure to write a comment too. (Human deaths require a private message.)

For better or worse (probably worse), the number of likes a post receives has become a shorthand measure of its success. As with follower counts, try not to get too caught up on this; it's easy to fall into the trap of constantly checking your feed after you post something, eagerly counting each little ping of validation as it comes in, but this will soon drive you to distraction.

Be generous with your own likes and gracious for those you receive. It's vulgar to 'chase' likes by posting things with

ALL THE THINGS A 'LIKE' CAN MEAN

I like this

I like you

Congratulations!

Well done!

This is funny

This is important

I am acknowledging that I have seen this

I think more people should see this

I want you to notice me

I agree with this

I don't agree with this, but you make some good points

I don't know what to say in response to this

I'm thinking of you

I have sympathy with you

I am expressing solidarity with you

I am your mother and it is my prerogative to like every single one of your posts the explicit goal of gaining interactions. In 2017, Facebook announced it would start demoting posts it classes as 'engagement bait', which includes posts that goad people into interacting with a post – 'Like if you think you're smarter than this!' – or that attempt to use likes and shares as a kind of voting system – 'Like if you love cats, share if you prefer dogs!'

The only major platform to have something like a 'dislike' button is Reddit, where users can 'downvote' posts as well as 'upvote' them. The balance of everyone's votes gives a kind of hive-mind assessment of whether the post is worth seeing or not. In 2015, Facebook also introduced a set of extra emoji 'reactions' to try to get around some of the ambiguity in a like. Beyond the original thumbs-up, you can now select one of five emoji icons in response to a post, labelled as 'love', 'haha', 'wow', 'sad' and 'angry'. Go easy on that last one – as we've covered, emoji aren't great at communicating nuance.

Finally, don't like your own posts – this is a bit sad, like trying to high-five yourself. And never like someone's break-up, even if you did think they weren't right for each other. It's awkward when they then get back together.

Shares and retweets

In the social media marketplace, a 'share' is worth more than a 'like'. By sharing someone's post on platforms that allow it, you're not just giving it a little algorithmic boost but directly promoting it to your friends or followers, therefore increasing its visibility.

On Twitter, retweets, or 'RTs', are a particularly valuable commodity, and people with high numbers of followers have great power when it comes to bestowing their precious shares on those with a more lowly reach. There's nothing more frustrating than seeing your witty tweet catch the eye of a Twitter celebrity, only for them to like but not retweet it. (Even worse are the people who still do the now-antiquated 'manual' retweet by writing 'RT @yourusername' and then copy-pasting the words of your tweet into their own post, thus crediting you enough to avoid accusations of plagiarism but keeping all of their followers' sweet likes and RTs for themselves.)

There are two types of retweet: a retweet without comment and a retweet with comment, also known as a 'quote tweet'. In the early days of Twitter, it was something of a trend for people to put 'RTs are not endorsements' in their bio. But let's get this clear: a straightforward RT can *only* really be interpreted as an endorsement. By hitting the retweet button, you are purposefully pushing the post to a wider audience, which, without further comment, must mean you think it deserving of wider distribution. The disclaimer does nothing to negate this; if you retweet something offensive, no one is going to check your bio and say, 'Oh but look, they say "RTs are not endorsements!" They're off the hook!' Instead, it just looks like a weak attempt to cover your arse if people disagree with you.

Be careful what you share, and never share links to stories you haven't actually read. If you do want to retweet something that you don't endorse – for example, in order to critique it – then you need to quote-tweet and add a note explaining your position.

The Ratio

Usually, a high number of interactions on social media is a good thing. If you get lots of likes and shares, that means lots of people have enjoyed your post. But *comments* can be another story. Comments on a post can be either positive or negative, and there's no way to tell just by looking at the numbers. Except there is. It's called The Ratio.

The concept of The Ratio took hold on Twitter around

2017. It's a simple rule: if the number of replies to a tweet vastly outweighs the number of likes or shares, then said tweet must be bad, wrong and/or morally repugnant.

The logic is that, if people agree with you, they will most likely hit 'like' or 'retweet', and perhaps comment as well (as a general rule, if you leave a positive comment on a post you should also like it). If many more people feel the need to dive into debate in the comments without hitting like or retweet, the post can't have been well received.

A prime example of The Ratio is found on a tweet posted to the verified United Airlines Twitter account in April 2017, in which CEO Oscar Munoz apologised following a viral video of a passenger being dragged off a flight. At the time of writing, Munoz's rather unsatisfactory apology for 'having to re-accommodate' the customer has 59,000 replies and just 7,300 likes. In Twitter parlance, he got thoroughly ratioed.

Tagging

The most direct way to get someone's attention on social media is to tag their username in a post or comment, which, depending on the circumstances, can be either a nice courtesy or a great irritant.

The one situation in which tagging is definitely necessary is to give credit. If you post a witty comment you didn't come up with, a joke you didn't devise or a picture you didn't take, you must tag the original source. Otherwise, it's just stealing. This is particularly important on Instagram, which, unlike Twitter and Facebook, doesn't let you directly share other people's posts into your main feed. Many get around this by using third-party 'regramming' apps or other workarounds, such as taking a screenshot. If you do this, make sure to include the original poster's name and handle.

You should also tag someone in a caption or comment if you are addressing them directly in a post – it's rude to talk about someone behind their back. Finally, you may wish to tag someone in a post or comment if you want to draw their attention to something. But only do this if you honestly, genuinely think they'll be interested; your motives should be considerate, and not self-serving.

Acceptable: tagging your best friend in the comments of an Instagram picture of a cute sloth, her favourite animal.

Unacceptable: tagging someone you've never met in a Twitter post promoting your startup.

Particular restraint is required when tagging people in images. It used to be that people would routinely tag every face in every picture in every album they uploaded to Facebook – and boy did we upload a lot of pictures back then. Our expectations of privacy have since changed, however, and we're now all a bit more wary about having photographic evidence of Friday night's antics online for all our crushes, in-laws and future employers to find. You should therefore always get permission from people before tagging them in an image. In fact, always get permission before you post photos of them on the internet full stop.

Hashtags

Hashtags have several main functions. The first is to categorise posts using keywords, so that other users who are interested in the same topic can find related content more easily. Someone posting an Instagram picture of a cake they made might use the hashtag #baking, so other keen bakers can see the fruits of their labour. Someone posting a tweet about this week's *Great British Bake Off* might use the hashtag #GBBO, so other viewers can see their opinion on whatever mean thing Paul Hollywood said this time. Hashtags can also unite people around more serious causes or express solidarity for a movement, such as #BlackLivesMatter or #MeToo.

Companies often try to tap into the hashtag phenomenon by inventing their own – with varying degrees of success. The problem is, once a hashtag has been cast out into the Twitter- or Instasphere, it is at the mercy of the social media masses, who don't always have the same idea for it as the company's marketing department intended. Notable missteps include #McDStories, which McDonalds introduced in 2012 for people to share stories about how much they loved the fast food chain, but which soon got flooded with tales of not-so-Happy Meals. Similarly, in 2014 the New York Police Department envisioned the public using its #MyNYPD hashtag to share warm-and-fuzzy photos of themselves with police officers, but it was soon hijacked by people sharing stories of police brutality instead. (At the time of writing, it mainly brings up tweets moaning about police cars apparently violating traffic rules.)

Another purpose of hashtags is to add semantic context to a post. Like emoji, a hashtag can add an emotional inflection or give the reader a clue as to how a post is meant to be read.

Time to get out of bed and head to the office
#MondayMotivation

has a very different meaning to

Time to get out of bed and head to the office
#ihatemondays

Just to confuse everyone, however, many people use hashtags ironically, so don't necessarily take them at face value.

The main etiquette around hashtags is not to go overboard; one or two is plenty. Adding a #hashtag to #every other #word in your #post makes it #difficulttoread and looks #spammyashell. Hashtag spamming is particularly rampant on Instagram, where people have a habit of tagging zillions of vaguely relevant words in an attempt to attract more followers. This is unlikely to make you more popular, but it almost definitely will make you look desperate.

A final word of warning: if you are inventing your own hashtag, be mindful of how it parses. Never forget that mirthful day in 2012 when singer Susan Boyle celebrated her album launch with the Twitter hashtag #Susanalbumparty. It was meant to read 'Susan album party', but many saw four words instead of three.

WHAT TO POST ON SOCIAL MEDIA
(AND WHEN TO STOP)

N OW WE GET to the crux of social media etiquette: what to actually post.

Try this mortifying trick. Go to your Facebook profile and under 'manage posts' select 'filters'. Scroll back to a date around the time you started using the site and, under 'posted by', select 'you'. Unless you've deleted them, this should take you back to some of your earliest ever Facebook posts.

If you're anything like me, you'll be faced with a wall full of thoroughly cringeworthy updates from around summer 2007. This was back when Facebook still encouraged you to narrate your life in the third person, with the prompt '[Your Name] *is*. . .' Cue a bunch of inane updates about your day, like '*Victoria is* eating dinner' or '*Victoria is* waiting for the bus' or '*Victoria is* wondering why homework has to be soooo annoying'. (Those are just made-up examples; the real ones are far too embarrassing to publish.)

You might also come across what look like private messages between you and your Facebook friends. Around this period, it was quite normal to write personal messages directly on friends' public Facebook walls for everyone to see – a habit that soon changed. By 2012, the idea of conducting a one-on-one conversation online in public seemed so alien that rumours started going around about a 'bug' in the site that had publicly exposed people's private inbox messages. Users thought they had been hacked, not realising that these were actually public wall posts all along and everyone just had a rather different idea of digital privacy back then.

Over time, norms changed. Facebook dropped the '*is*' in status updates, and we no longer felt the need to let all of our contacts know the minutiae of whatever we happened to be doing, thinking or eating for breakfast (that's what Instagram was invented for). Image and video posts became more common, and news-sharing on social media became a much more widespread phenomenon, bringing a new dynamic to the news feed.

Different platforms are geared towards slightly different uses. Facebook today is mainly a place to get angry about current affairs, watch cute videos and occasionally update your mother on what's going on in your life. Twitter, with its 280-character limit, is suited to short, pithy posts and back-and-forth exchanges between users, with fast-moving debate often responsive to news cycles. Platforms such as Instagram, Snapchat and Pinterest, meanwhile, differentiate themselves by being almost exclusively image-focused.

When it comes to composing a post, Debrett's has some pretty solid advice on the subject of 'social tact' which I can't help but think is as relevant to social media as to any high-society dinner party: '*You may be someone who disdains political correctness, but racist, sexist or homophobic remarks are unacceptable in any circumstances. You may think you are being funny but it is best to keep humour under control.*'

A note on privacy

Before you do post something, take a few minutes to look over your privacy settings. No reasonable person could expect you to go through every social media site's complete T&Cs (many contain around the same number of words as this chapter and are, I hope, much less fun to read), but you should at least check who can see what you post. On many platforms, you can choose whether to make posts public by default, or keep them visible only to people you're connected with. It's better to find out now than when your boss likes that beach-break selfie you posted while you were 'off sick'.

Remember, however, that the internet doesn't forget and, even with carefully configured privacy settings, your posts could easily end up in front of a wider audience than you anticipate. Dance like no one's watching, sing like no one's listening, but post online like everything you write could one day be read by your boss, your mother or a court of law.

Posting frequency

There's a fine line between keeping your friends and followers regularly updated and spamming. Post too often and you'll be that annoying friend who clogs up everyone else's feeds; post too little and your mum will complain that she has no idea what's going on in your life any more.

Exactly how often you should post corresponds roughly to how ephemeral the platform is. You should post less on platforms like Facebook, where posts can hang around in the news feed for a while, than on Twitter, where tweets soon get buried by fresher fare. By the same token, you should be more selective with the photos and videos you post on your main Instagram feed than on your Instagram or Snapchat Story, where they disappear after 24 hours.

There's no set rule for the maximum amount you should post, but my rule of thumb is:

Facebook	1 post per day
Instagram	1 post per day (but can include multiple photos in one post)
LinkedIn	1 post per day
Twitter	10 posts per day
Instagram/ Snapchat Story	10 posts per day (but *only* if you have lots of interesting things to share, like if you're on holiday)

These are *maximums*. Don't feel like you *need* to post if you don't have something to share. We're not going to call the Missing Persons Unit if your Instagram isn't updated every day.

Image posts

Over the past decade, images have become much more important on social media, and our approach to posting photos has also evolved. The emphasis is now firmly on quality over

A-Z OF INSTAGRAM CLICHÉS

A is for aerial views of avocado toast

B is for #blessed

C is for circle of feet

D is for 'doing it for the 'gram'

E is for eggs (and other breakfast foods)

F is for FOMO

G is for graffiti wall

H is for hand heart

I is for influencer

J is for jumping for joy!

K is for Kardashians

L is for ledge, dangerously perched on

M is for 'mood'

N is for #nofilter

O is for ocean view

P is for plane window

Q is for (inspirational) quote

R is for Rich Kids of Instagram

S is for 'sound on'

T is for #throwbackthursday

U is for unicorn pool inflatable

V is for vintage

W is for weddings, weddings and more weddings

X is for your ex who likes every selfie

Y is for yoga poses

Z is for zealous use of zoom-ins in your Instagram Story

quantity. No longer is it acceptable to upload a whole album of holiday snaps to Facebook; you need to curate that one picture-perfect shot for Instagram (because if you come back from holiday without hashtagging a #sunset, did you really go away at all?).

Dave Burt, CEO and founder of social media agency Be Global Social, says the key to a successful account is curation. And he should know – he runs the popular @London Instagram account, which has more than 2 million followers and a billion total views. If you're trying to attract a following, Burt advises finding your brand and sticking to it. The @London account is about celebrating London, and that's exactly what it does, with pictures of landmarks, art and food around the city. Iconic landmarks such as Big Ben and Tower Bridge routinely perform well, but variety is also crucial. 'If you post a picture of Tower Bridge seven days a week, people get bored of that,' Burt says. The same goes for your selfies, bikini shots and pictures of brunch.

Put some thought into lighting and composition. Think about things like the 'rule of thirds' – arranging objects in your photo as if they're in a 3x3 grid, which often produces a pleasing aesthetic. Only use filters if they actually enhance your image, not just as a gimmick. Putting your whole feed in Gingham doesn't make you some kind of kooky artist, it just makes all your pictures look washed out.

Selfies

Selfies get a lot of flak – *they're narcissistic, they're vain, they're self-indulgent* – but we all love them really. A paper by researchers at Georgia Tech and Yahoo Labs that looked at 1 million Instagram posts found that photos containing a face were 38 per cent more likely to be 'liked' than photos that didn't, and 32 per cent more likely to attract a comment.[3] And before you assume that these results may have been skewed by a few super-hot subjects posting thirst traps, know that the age and gender of the person or people in the photo didn't affect how much people engaged with it.

This makes sense to me: I follow people on Instagram primarily because I want to see what's going on in my friends' personal lives, not an endless stream of latte art – and what's more personal than a picture of yourself? Just don't overdo it. Not every photo should be a selfie. And don't take yourself too seriously – it's OK to smile sometimes.

Seven selfie archetypes

If selfies are a means of self-expression, we're not a particularly original bunch. Here are some common examples you'll no doubt see pop up in your feed.

The thirst trap

Thirst traps are knowingly designed to be sexy as hell, with the express purpose of attracting attention – and the likes that come with it. They often feature a lot of skin, 'duck face' expressions and as much nipple as Instagram will let you get away with (which, to be fair, isn't much). The gym selfie also falls into this category.

The no make-up selfie

The idea behind the no make-up selfie trend was to empower women by rebelling against unrealistic beauty standards – which might have worked better if it wasn't mainly embraced by people who already have perfect bone structure, flawless skin and lip fillers. #iwokeuplikethis

The ugly selfie

Unlike the actually-still-very-attractive no make-up selfie, the ugly selfie is purposefully unflattering. The fatter your double chins, the goofier your teeth and the more scrunched-up your nose, the better. The ugly selfie is meant as an antidote to the perfectly posed portraits in most of your Instagram uploads.

The fashion selfie

The fashion selfie is unusual in that it's full-length, the better to show off your #ootd (outfit of the day). This means you usually have to rope some other poor sod into taking the picture so you can prance about finding your best angles – making its status as a selfie debatable. Just make sure to carefully hide the tags on everything so you can return them for a refund once you've got the right shot. . .

The emo selfie

Before there was Instagram, there was Myspace, and though the early social media platform may have since floundered, it left behind an unmistakeable aesthetic: the emo selfie. Trademarks include the 'Myspace angle' (camera held aloft and to the side) and copious amounts of hairspray. Bonus points if you take it with an actual digital camera, not a phone.

The arty selfie

The arty selfie is for people who think they're far too sophisticated for selfies yet still can't resist the lure of the front-facing camera. Moody lighting is a must, as are a few highbrow accessories, like a stack of books carefully positioned as if they just happened to get caught in shot. What do you mean, you don't always carry a copy of *Infinite Jest* around with you?

The belfie

Possibly the only selfie where your face isn't the anatomical focus, the 'belfie' is a selfie in which your posterior takes pride of place ('belfie' referring to a 'bum selfie'). You don't need to be a contortionist to take one: just position yourself in front of a mirror, clench those buttocks and take the shot over your shoulder. You're welcome.

'Candid' shots

Almost more common than selfies on social media these days are faux-candid shots, sometimes known as 'plandids' (for 'planned candid'). This apparent oxymoron refers to pictures that are presented as if they were just snapped in the moment, but that we all know you actually spent at least 10 minutes trying to perfectly position yourself for, your boyfriend-slash-obligatory-personal-photographer taking a whole roll of pictures until he got that one where the breeze was lifting your hair just so.

Plandids usually catch the subject in a not-at-all-obviously-staged pose, like sitting on a beach in a spontaneous yoga position or staring wistfully at the horizon (don't you just find yourself doing that all the time?). Another favourite is the 'follow me' pose – a picture of you from behind, with one hand stretched back towards the photographer. It's just a totally natural and not-at-all-awkward way to hold hands.

If you're single and too mortified to ask someone else to take 2,000 shots of you in your bikini until you get one that flatters all of your wobbly bits, then you can take a plandid with the help of your phone's timer. Pro tip: use your camera's burst mode. Getting that perfect 'gram is a numbers game.

Food photography

Food photography on social media was never that notice-able until Instagram came along, and something about that square-shaped frame apparently brainwashed us all into thinking we were restaurant critics. Now, it's rare to enjoy a meal out without spotting someone with their phone floating over their plate.

The main rule of food photos is that the food itself must look appetising. Your lovingly homemade lasagne might taste great, but if it looks more like a dog's dinner than fine dining, there's only so much a filter can do. Take care when plating to make a composition that looks interesting. It is the law that food photos must be taken from overhead.

Breakfast and brunch foods are especially popular on Instagram, to the extent that it's now incredibly passé to post pictures of smashed avocado or eggs on toast, no matter how deliciously oozy you've got the yolks. And please don't post pictures of healthy foods, like salads or those abominable green smoothies – we want to see food porn, not sanctimoni-ous reminders of how disgustingly healthy you are.

If you're taking pictures of food while eating out, remem-ber your table manners and be considerate of fellow diners. It's acceptable to take one shot of a particularly good-looking dish, but not to spend half the evening hovering out of your chair to get that perfect aerial view.

Stories

Snapchat, Instagram and Facebook all have 'Stories' channels now, which are separate to your main feed and let you post a series of photos and videos that disappear after 24 hours. This means you can share extra moments from your day without clogging up people's feeds with multiple posts.

Stories usually have a more personal, 'behind the scenes' feel. Think actually candid, not plandid. Stories also let you add text, stickers and animated filters to your posts. Text can be helpful to explain what's going on in a picture, but keep it snappy. Remember that each clip in a Story only displays for 10 seconds unless you hold your finger on it, and there's nothing more annoying than trying to race through a long description only for the next post to flash up before you reach the end. If you include video clips, avoid relying on audio, as many people browse with the sound turned off.

Oh, and shooting Story posts in landscape orientation is a social media cardinal sin.

Memes

Photos aren't the only kind of image post. There's another sort, and it spreads like wildfire. I'm talking, of course, about memes.

Think of a meme and the first thing to spring to mind is probably an image overlaid with some kind of amusing text, most likely in white, bold Impact font. Maybe it's a cat asking, 'I can has cheezburger?' or a frustrated Boromir from *Lord of the Rings* wisely imparting that 'One does not simply walk into Mordor.' These kind of memes, known as image macros, are just the tip of the iceberg.

The word 'meme' was coined by evolutionary biologist

Richard Dawkins in his book *The Selfish Gene*. Dawkins explains in his book that he settled on the word as 'a noun that conveys the idea of a unit of cultural transmission, or a unit of *imitation*' (his emphasis). He was not talking specifically about digital culture; *The Selfish Gene* was originally published in 1976, a full 13 years before the creation of the World Wide Web, so we can safely assume that he had never come across a lolcat by that point. Rather, Dawkins wrote, memes are anything that propagates by 'leaping from brain to brain', such as 'tunes, ideas, catch-phrases, clothes fashions, ways of making pots or of building arches'. It was only after the internet became commercial that people began to apply the idea of memes to digital content.

These days, memes are often associated with images, though they can be anything – videos, songs, texts, catch-phrases or more nebulous behaviours. Limor Shifman, an associate professor at the Hebrew University of Jerusalem who has studied internet memes and published a book on her findings, *Memes in Digital Culture*, says that there's a difference between a meme and something that just 'goes viral'. A piece of content goes viral when it is seen and shared by many people. A meme, however, not only gets shared but is also adapted along the way – remade and remixed again and again to produce endless variations. This is where Dawkins's 'unit of *imitation*' definition comes in.

To take an example: 'Gangnam Style', the 2012 runaway hit by South Korean artist PSY, is a viral music video; it now has over 3.2 billion views on YouTube. But what makes it a *meme* is the fact that people have made their own versions, imitating the dancing or creating parody videos.

Schifman says that the reason we love memes so much is because they allow us to express ourselves both as an individual and as part of a collective. 'When I create my version of a popular video, I simultaneously convey my individuality – this is my body, my sense of humour, my talent – and some communality to a shared core,' she explains. Memes can also help form a kind of in-group language, with specific online communities adopting memes that outsiders don't understand, to help establish a group identity.

Some memes enjoy abrupt but short-lived popularity, while others stick around for years. The ones that last longest are often very versatile and appeal to some kind of core human sentiment. Schifman gives the example of Success Kid, an image macro that features a baby boy clenching a handful of sand in a way that makes it look like he's doing a celebratory fist pump. This image first became a meme around 2007, with people adding text that usually centres around celebrating a minor victory. More than ten years later, it's still going strong. 'Success Kid is still around because this notion of being successful in trying conditions is still appealing,' Schifman says.

And while memes are often used as jokes, they can have more serious contexts. Memes are increasingly used in politics and activism, or to raise awareness of social issues. Schifman gives the example of the #MeToo movement. '#MeToo is a very good example of a meme that is both personal and political,' she says. 'When a woman posts a Facebook post or a tweet about her own sexual harassment, she simultaneously says something personal about herself, but at the same time she pinpoints a broad political problem that relates to inequality and injustice.'

How to make a meme (if you must)

As with gifs, you can find repositories of memes online, which you can share or adapt at will. If you're feeling creative, you can even make your own. Image macros are among the easiest to make. All you have to do is take an image, add a witty caption and *voilà,* you've made a meme. (Well, you've made an image macro, which, if you're lucky, may take off as a meme.)

There are many web-based tools that do a lot of the work for you, such as Imgur's and Imgflip's meme generators. These sites let you choose from a selection of common meme images or upload your own, and then prompt you to enter text in a template so that it appears in the right place over the image. When you're done, hit 'generate meme' and there you have it.

There are a few different types of image macro, including 'Advice Animals', which present an animal or personality as a kind of stock character (Boromir and Success Kid come under this category) and 'object labelling memes', where certain parts of the image are labelled to comic effect, as in the 'distracted boyfriend' or 'expanding brain' memes. If you have no idea what I'm talking about, the KnowYourMeme database is a great resource for translating whatever weird craze has taken hold of the internet by the time you're reading this book. Just keep a few pointers in mind before you start sharing your own meme creations:

Know your audience. Some memes are self-explanatory, but others require prior knowledge to make any sense. Stick to the classics if you're posting in an environment where others may not be entirely *au fait* with the latest meme trend. Or, of course, you can try a niche take on a common meme – though this can get boring when your feeds are filled with dozens of versions of the same image, each featuring its own in-joke.

Stick to the template. Memes rely on shared context to be understood. Mess with the template and suddenly you've got a Socially Awkward Penguin (a penguin on a blue background, facing left) instead of a Socially Awesome Penguin (the same penguin on a red background, facing right). Awkward.

Make sure you understand the meme. That weird-looking cartoon frog? That's Pepe, and while he used to be known for his catchphrase 'Feels good man', he's now become associated with alt-right ideology. One to avoid.

Don't turn real people into memes. Public figures are fair game, but don't try to turn someone you know into a meme, as it might end up haunting them. I'm sure Scumbag Steve is a lovely person really.

HOW (NOT) TO BEHAVE ON SOCIAL MEDIA

Now we've covered the basics, it's time to dig our teeth into some of the more nuanced manners and problematic behaviours when it comes to digital etiquette and online communities. Because while social media can help forge connections to share wisdom and support, it can also bring out the worst in people. From minor irritants to genuine societal concerns, here are some of things you should *avoid* doing.

A non-exhaustive list of all the annoying people you know on social media

Everyone can count the below among their social media connections. Just make sure it's not you.

The oversharer

Over-sharing can come in many forms. It's the multi-paragraph feelings dump you should really be saving for your therapist, the kissy-emoji PDAs between you and your new partner and the TMI when you recount in detail your recent colonoscopy. Save it for your personal diary. We really, really don't need to know.

Example: *'So just got back from the doctor. Anyone got a recommendation for a good haemorrhoid cream?'*

The inspirational quoter

This is the person who thinks that posting inspirational quotes and motivational messages, usually against a backdrop of a whimsical nature photo, makes them look clever or 'deep'. These quotes usually don't make much sense, reading more like a badly translated fortune cookie than real words of wisdom, and are often implausibly attributed to Albert Einstein or Mark Twain. Inspirational quoters may have the best of intentions, but the only thing they really inspire you to do is to punch your computer screen.

Example: *'Every great dream begins with a dreamer'* – *Albert Einstein. Soooo true, words to live by <3*

The armchair activist

It's all very well having an opinion on politics, but there's always someone who sees everyone else's news feeds as their own personal soapbox. They insist that they're all about political debate but seem to have no interest in actually hearing other people's views. They'll often post media stories with comments like 'This is what the media isn't talking about,' without a shred of irony. They constantly badger you to sign online petitions, but they wouldn't have a clue what to do at an actual protest.

Example: *'Sign this petition if you think saving lives is more important than watching* Love Island, *I guess reality TV is more important than actual reality to most people these days.'*

The fitness fanatic

This is the person for whom social media is simply a place to record their sporting prowess. Whether they're a marathon runner or a gym bunny, they treat their posts like entries in *Bridget Jones's Diary*, except for instead of tracking alcohol and cigarettes they're always going on about things like 'PBs' and 'gains'. They have their Fitbit connected wirelessly so that they don't even have to log on to show up how inadequate the rest of us are.

Example: *'Just a gentle run this morning before work, only 20 miles today! Don't forget to sponsor me on GoFundMe for my 17th marathon of the year!'*

The consummate quizzer

Pretty much all this person posts is the results of random internet quizzes. They can tell you off the top of their head which Hogwarts house they're in, which Disney princess they are, and which novelty ice cream flavour best represents their personality. Not content with performing this kind of BuzzFeed psychoanalysis just on themselves, they like to tag all of their friends to encourage them to take the quiz too.

Example: *'Which kitchen utensil are you? I got: potato masher. OMG this is so accurate, I am such a masher! @Sally you should try this, I bet you're a spatula!'*

The Debbie Downer

Like a real-life Moaning Myrtle, all this person does is *complain*. About their job, about their relationship, about the poor customer service they received at Tesco this afternoon – the most minor thing can set them off on a public rant that sucks all the joy out of your social media feed. Reading through their posts, you'd be forgiven for thinking they're the only person who has to deal with such inconveniences as Monday mornings, monthly bills and miserable weather.

Example: *'Can't believe my boss actually expects me to do work at work, it's so unfair. Why does he get to tell me what to do anyway?'*

The 'I'm leaving social media' prima donna

Observable evidence may point to the contrary, but it is in fact possible to stop using social media without making a big announcement about it – *on social media*, no less. Like think-pieces on 'Why I'm leaving London' or magazine columns on 'What happened when I gave up my smartphone for a day', it's not new, it's not special, and we're all fed up of hearing about it. It's fine to decide not to use social media, but you don't have to act all smug about it. It's a personal lifestyle choice, not some great moral conundrum.

Example: *'So, after a lot of deliberation, I've decided to take the difficult (but ultimately, I believe, noble) step of leaving social media. The main reason is that I think people on social media spend way too much time obsessing about themselves. In the following 2,000-word essay, I'll explain why I'm different. . .'*

SOCIAL MEDIA BEHAVIOURS
THAT NEED TO DIE

BEYOND THE IRRITATING personalities we all know and endure are some more insidious and malicious behaviours that make everyone's online experience that bit worse.

Vaguebooking

Although initially coined in reference to Facebook posts, 'vaguebooking' can be observed on all social media sites. The term refers to the phenomenon whereby someone writes a post that is intentionally vague in order to get attention.

Vaguebooking posts are often emotional in nature but omit the cause of the poster's angst, forcing their concerned friends to comment 'What's up hun???' and 'U ok???' Vaguebookers are the kind of people who regularly use Facebook's emoji stickers to update friends on their (usually negative) feelings. Their posts often end in an ellipsis, just in case you didn't realise that they actually have more they want to say. . .

Subtweeting

Subtweeting is to Twitter what vaguebooking is to Facebook. In this case, the part of the post that remains vague is the subject. In a subtweet, the poster is clearly referring to a specific person but doesn't directly tag their username or mention their name.

People usually subtweet when they want to criticise or mock someone but aren't brave enough to do it to their face. It's basically the Twitter version of bitching about someone behind their back.

Subtweeting is acceptable if you're talking about a public figure, or if you know that mentioning the person by name would lead to a pile-on from their angry followers. In other cases, it is simply rude; if you believe you have a valid critique of someone's behaviour, you should at least be prepared to let them respond.

Bragging, humblebragging and inspiring FOMO

Social media is made for showing off, but you should at least try to be subtle about it.

Bragging on social media can take many forms. It's posting a zillion perfect photos of your perfect life on Instagram, or tweeting only about your own achievements. It's using the 'check in' function on Facebook to let everyone know which exotic new location you're in today, often before you've even left the airport. (A recent alternative to the check-in is to ask for 'recommendations' in a new city, framing a brag as a genuine request for help. Don't be fooled: people who do this don't *really* need your suggestions for cocktails in Rio de Janeiro; they just want you to know that they are having cocktails in Rio de Janeiro.)

Worse than straight-up bragging, however, is humblebragging – the art of bragging while pretending to do the opposite. A humblebrag is an ostensibly self-deprecating post that is in fact clearly just a front for showing off how great you are and how amazing your life is. Humblebrags can come in text or picture form and often have an air of 'first world problem' about them – you're just *too* successful, *too* wealthy, *too* skinny, *too* smart.

'OMG I'm so clumsy, I just tripped on my way onstage to collect an award!' says the humblebragger. 'LOL just spilled coffee on my new Chanel dress – and it was so hard to find one in a size zero!' they complain. 'Ugh, jet lag sucks,' they comment on an Instagram picture of them lazing on a pristine beach in Bora Bora. And yes, it still counts as bragging if you put #blessed at the end.

All of this boasting contributes to the feeling of FOMO, or 'fear of missing out' – the assumption we all make that everyone else is living a much more interesting, exciting life than we are, because all we see are their carefully curated social media posts. Just remember that, in reality, they probably have just as many lonely evenings, disappointing meals and bad hair days as you do. Probably.

Mansplaining

Ah, mansplaining. As if it didn't happen enough in real life, mansplaining has truly found its spiritual home in online communities of every variety.

Mansplaining is when someone (usually a man) explains something to someone else (usually a woman) in a patronising manner that insults their intelligence. The phenomenon is epitomised in Rebecca Solnit's 2008 essay *Men Explain Things to Me*, which opens with the author recounting the time a man at a party tried to explain one of her own books to her. Solnit didn't actually coin the term 'mansplaining', but the word soon caught on to describe a practice that resonated with many women.

It's important to clarify that mansplaining is not just a man explaining something. Mansplaining is necessarily condescending, based on the mansplainer's assumption that the person they are talking to can't possibly be as clever

ARE YOU MANSPLAINING?

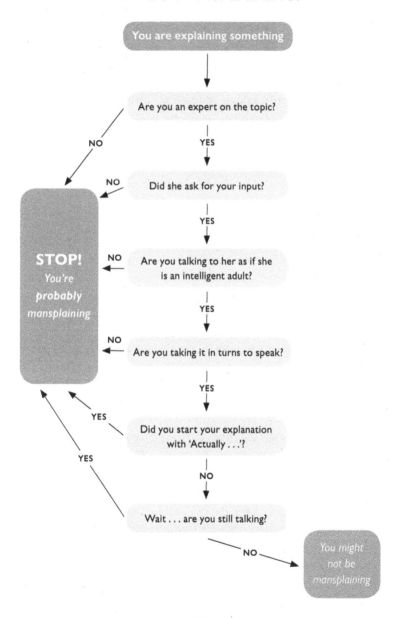

or knowledgeable as they are – even when all the evidence suggests as much. Mansplaining is a dude who once read *A Brief History of Time* trying to explain black holes to an astrophysicist, or someone who watched last night's *Masterchef* outlining the finer points of chocolate tempering to a professional pastry chef. Some men are true masters of the form, nobly and selflessly taking it upon themselves to mansplain to women on such topics as feminism or childbirth. And who said chivalry was dead?

Tweetstorming

Speaking of mansplaining. . . Twitter threads, also known as tweetstorms, are when you write multiple tweets on the same subject in rapid succession and 'thread' them together by replying each time to the tweet before, so that you end up with a chain of connected posts. Threads are a way of getting around Twitter's 280-character limit. More often than not, they're also just incredibly obnoxious. And I'd bet my last Rolo that the Venn diagram between habitual mansplainers and tweetstormers is essentially a circle.

By posting a long Twitter thread, you're basically asserting your dominance over your followers by insisting on taking up more than the usual allotted space. Everyone else gets 280 characters, but what *you* have to say is worth ten times that. In an article for tech site Gizmodo, writer Alana Hope Levinson compares tweetstorming to 'manspreading' – when men sit on public transport with their legs spread wide open, taking up their own designated leg room plus that of their neighbours. She invents the term 'manthreading' and describes those who embark on lengthy Twitter threads as 'people who want their ideas to take up the absolute most space possible. Like Manspreading, but of digital space.'[4]

It's not that people who write Twitter threads don't occasionally have something interesting to say; it's that they're forcing it into an inappropriate medium. If you want to write an essay, why choose a platform that only lets you post a sentence at a time? Levinson suggests that manthreaders are particularly attracted to Twitter threads because it gives the illusion that they're coming up with each point on the spur of the moment, firing off zinger after zinger as if they haven't painstakingly prepared the whole thread in advance (spoiler: they have). 'They want constant kudos for each point, a stream of high fives for each of their killer "owns",' she writes.

Don't be that guy. If you can't quite fit everything you want to say in a tweet, then a two- or three-part thread is fine, but more than that and you should probably just save it for that imaginary TED Talk you're clearly dying to give.

FIVE SIGNS YOUR TWITTER THREAD IS TOO LONG:

- You have the whole thing written out in a Word doc before you start tweeting
- You have to number the entries so people don't lose track
- You feel the need to preface the thread with 'THREAD'
- You provide footnotes
- You mention 'game theory' at any point

Public shaming

Some people just revel in others' misfortune. Public shaming is when a person publicly calls out someone else's behaviour in order to humiliate them, usually with the goal of damaging their career or reputation.

The canonical example of public shaming is the case of Justine Sacco. In 2013, Sacco, a communications executive, was on her way to South Africa. Before she boarded the plane, she tweeted, 'Going to Africa. Hope I don't get AIDS. Just kidding. I'm white!' The tweet soon spread past Sacco's handful of followers to become a trending topic on Twitter. Scores of strangers began calling for her to be fired, using the #HasJustineLandedYet hashtag (Sacco had turned her phone off for the flight). She lost her job as a result.

While it's acceptable – even laudable – to call out discrimination, be wary of revelling in this kind of online schadenfreude without knowing all the facts. Social media posts can easily be taken out of context, and the snap judgement of the digital masses means reactions can soon snowball out of proportion. In Sacco's case, the tweet was apparently meant as a joke – an ironic take on what an ignorant racist might say. It was a *bad* joke, but surely not bad enough to warrant quite that level of ensuing vitriol.

These days, public shaming has become a kind of rite of passage for anyone who gains some kind of public attention. Sometimes, this is justified: the public has a right to know if a newly appointed politician, for example, has a history of espousing racist or homophobic views. But sometimes, public shaming appears to be little more than a weapon of harassment, designed to bully someone into silence rather than to genuinely critique their behaviour.

Milkshake Duck

Related to public shaming, a 'Milkshake Duck' describes someone who suddenly enters the public eye and becomes immediately well-loved on social media, before falling out of favour just as quickly after unsavoury details about them are uncovered. The term was coined by comedy Twitter account @pixelatedboat, which tweeted in 2016: 'The whole internet loves Milkshake Duck, a lovely duck that drinks milkshakes! *5 seconds later* We regret to inform you the duck is racist'.

A good example of a real-life Milkshake Duck is Ken Bone, the 'undecided voter' who won hearts with his woolly red jumper and neighbourly demeanour when he asked a question during one of the 2016 televised US presidential debates. Bone became a social media darling overnight, only to get Milkshake Ducked a short while after, when people found questionable content in his Reddit history.

IRL eavesdropping

If shaming people for their online behaviour weren't intrusive enough, it's become a kind of meme in recent years to eavesdrop on strangers' conversations and then broadcast them on social media for people to laugh at, such as live-tweeting someone's awkward first date or messy breakup. It usually starts something like: 'Wow so the couple in the next apartment is having the craziest breakup fight right now. THREAD!'

This is highly invasive, very creepy and shows a severe lack of both online and offline manners – not to mention that you likely have no idea what's really going on in people's lives. In September 2018, a video made the rounds on the internet of a man shaving his beard on a train out of New York. People readily mocked him, only for him to come forward and explain that he'd just left a homeless shelter and was trying to clean up to visit his family. Have some compassion, and don't stick your phone into other people's business.

Fake news, and how to spot it

If you want evidence that behaviour in the digital world can have an impact beyond the world behind our computer screens, look no further than the scourge of fake news.

News-sharing has become very prevalent on social media. Scroll through your news feeds today and you'll likely see just as many links to stories from media outlets as you will personal updates. The most recent Digital News Report by the Reuters Institute for the Study of Journalism at the University of Oxford, published in 2018, found that 39 per cent of people in the UK had used social media as a news source in the preceding week. Facebook was by far the largest contributor, with 27 per cent saying they had used it as a news source in the past week.[5]

Social media's role as a news source has been linked to the spread of fake news, with Facebook in particular coming in for criticism after it was uncovered that accounts linked to Russia had attempted to use the platform to influence US voters ahead of the 2016 presidential election.

What counts as fake news? The term has taken on something of a life of its own, being bandied around these days to mean anything from allegations of media bias to whatever Donald Trump doesn't like. In reality, neither of these is strictly fake news. For something to be fake news, it has to be:

a) News – it must be presented as fact.

b) Fake – as in, the information must be demonstrably not true.

Opinions don't count, however strongly you disagree with them, and there's a difference between something being poorly conceived and factually incorrect.

Fake news is not an honest mistake; it is deliberately designed to mislead, usually to support a political agenda or for financial gain. In the most extreme cases, it can involve full-on conspiracy theories, fabricated wholesale. In 2016, a conspiracy theory known as 'pizzagate' went viral, which alleged that individuals close to the Hillary Clinton presidential campaign were involved in a child abuse ring that operated out of a pizza restaurant in Washington, DC (the evidence included such convincing proof as 'maybe "cheese pizza" is a code word for "child pornography"'). The absurdity of the conspiracy might have been laughable, if it weren't for the fact that people actually believed it and hounded the restaurant staff with threats of violence and death. Eventually, one man decided to check it out for himself – armed with an assault rifle. Luckily, in that case no one was hurt.

Not all fake news is so obvious, and these stories are purposely designed to appeal to specific biases or worldviews, which makes them highly share-able. Before you get lured into spreading something that may be fake news, stop and ask yourself these six questions:

1. Have you read the story?

It's too easy to share a compelling-sounding story without actually reading it, but a headline emphasises the most attention-grabbing aspect and may not accurately reflect the full contents. Check that the evidence in the piece backs it up.

2. Where is it published?

If you don't know the publication, take a closer look. Are the writing and design up to the standard you'd expect? Does the journalist have a professional profile on social media? Check the site's mission to see if it is affiliated with a particular person, movement or viewpoint that might affect its perspective.

3. Do the sources check out?

A good journalist will always make it clear where they have got their information. Do some research on the sources quoted – are they legitimate authorities on the subject? Click on any links offered as evidence to see if they really do support the story.

4. Is it just a bit too amazing/surprising/outrageous?

Extraordinary claims require extraordinary evidence, so anything that feels a bit too much should set your spidey sense tingling. Fake news is often designed to outrage, so be extra conscientious if something has got your blood boiling.

5. What do the fact-checkers say?

Sites like Snopes and factcheck.org regularly debunk fake news and conspiracy theories. Check if this story is a known hoax. If it's a bombshell of a story and no mainstream outlets are running it, that's usually a sign that it doesn't meet general reporting standards.

6. Is it satire?

Finally, don't be that person who accidentally shares an article by satire sites such as The Onion or The Daily Mash thinking it's real. (And if you do, don't pretend you were 'just seeing if any of my friends would fall for it lol'. We all see you.)

If you do accidentally share a story you later learn is fake, don't leave it up, as this may only cause it to propagate further. Your best option is transparency. Delete the post, and let any friends or followers know that you have removed it after learning it was not true.

Fake images

There's a popular retort on internet forums when someone makes an improbable claim: 'Pics or it didn't happen.' But photographic evidence isn't always foolproof.

Every time there's a hurricane or other extreme weather event, a familiar image starts doing the rounds: a shark, casually swimming down a flooded highway road. The image is completely fake. The picture of the shark was originally captured by conservation photographer Thomas P. Peschak in 2003, during a trip to South Africa with scientists from the White Shark Trust. But Peschak's photo is very different to the 'shark on a highway' version; in the original, the shark is shown in stunning blue ocean following a kayaker, not swimming alongside cars in muddy floodwater. The latter is a work of pure imagination (and Photoshop).

If an image seems unlikely to be real, you can try doing a reverse image search using Google or TinEye to see if the picture has appeared elsewhere previously. Be particularly wary in the aftermath of natural disasters or terrorist incidents, which tend to attract hoaxes. One particularly heinous trend has seen trolls post fake images of people they claim are missing following school shootings and other attacks.

As AI technology advances, even videos aren't necessarily all they seem, with synthesised videos – known as 'deepfakes'

– superimposing one image onto another to mislead the viewer, for example making it look as if someone is saying or doing something they are not.

Filter bubbles and echo chambers

Fake news isn't the only perceived threat social media presents to our understanding of the world. The idea of the 'filter bubble' refers to the fact that what we see online – including what appears in our search results and social media feeds – is influenced by algorithms that personalise the information they serve us based on what they think we want to see. This has led to concerns that our experience on social media is an 'echo chamber' – i.e. that we only see posts we are likely to agree with and are therefore not exposed to other points of view.

The filter bubble is often evoked in reference to political events such as the election of Donald Trump and the outcome of the UK's EU referendum, to explain why so many people felt taken by surprise at these results. *How could so many people vote for Brexit when everyone in my Facebook feed was against it?*

It's certainly true that social media sites mediate what we see and how we see it, and that there's a concerning lack of transparency around how their algorithms work. But it's hard to judge to what extent these algorithms cause a filter bubble or echo chamber effect beyond what we would experience regardless. The biggest effect on your newsfeed is likely to be down to the people you connect with, who, as in the offline world, are probably likely to share similar views to you anyway.

William Dutton, professor emeritus at the University of Southern California, thinks that fears around social media echo chambers are overhyped, and argues that social media can actually expose us to a more diverse range of opinions.

'Certainly it's very clear in my case that my Facebook friends are far more heterogeneous than my friends in real life, in my neighbourhood or in my workplace,' he says.

The best way to counter your echo chamber, Dutton says, is to be aware of the issue. Make sure you're getting your news from multiple sources; if you're interested in a story you see on social media, search for information on it elsewhere, too. Don't cull your social networks of people who have different views, but instead try to engage with their opinions. 'Celebrate the fact that you know people and are open-minded to multiple points of view,' he says.

TROLLING

WHILE THE BEHAVIOURS we've covered up to here could feasibly stem from good intentions, trolling is committed with the express purpose of causing disruption.

The term 'trolling' has come to describe a broad range of behaviours, from your mate Rickrolling you to armies of bots waging targeted campaigns of harassment. Lucas Dixon is chief research scientist at Google's Jigsaw, which is developing AI tools to help detect and moderate toxic comments on internet forums. He says a definition is hard to pinpoint. 'Usually, trolling has some element of repeated behaviour; it's not a one-off,' he says. 'But apart from that, there's not much else that nails this term down.'

Trolls usually aim to disrupt a conversation, cause conflict or provoke an emotional reaction. Indeed, when you think of the origin of the term 'trolling', you might think of the folkloric monster that hides under bridges and causes mischief, but, while the analogy may be quite apt, some suggest that the word actually comes from a fishing technique. When you 'troll' for fish, you bait a line and draw it through the water, waiting for them to bite – just like the internet troll dropping an incendiary remark and waiting for someone to rise to the bait.

Trolls can have different motives. They may want to cause actual distress, they may want to make a political point, they may want to waste your time, or they may just be doing it for the lulz (for a laugh).

COMMON TROLL SPECIES

Given that the word 'trolling' can refer to many different behaviours, here are some of the more common types you might come across.

The prankster

The prankster trolls for a laugh – although his sense of humour may differ substantially from that of polite society. Common online pranks include bait-and-switch tricks, where the troll dupes the viewer into clicking a joke link (as in Rickrolling); advice trolling, where the troll offers to help someone but then gives them false advice for their own amusement; and old-fashioned practical jokes, which are often captured for posterity on YouTube.

The hacktivist

Some groups use trolling as a means to make a political point – for example, to raise awareness about an issue, produce satirical content or launch politically motivated online attacks. A well-known example is Anonymous, which has employed trolling antics against targets including ISIS and the Church of Scientology.

The concern troll

The concern troll pretends to align themselves with one side of a debate when in reality they hold the opposing view. They use their position as an infiltrator to voice false 'concerns' in an attempt to derail and undermine discussion. For example, a concern troll might pose as a feminist but then raise concerns about the way a feminist campaign is being conducted. One of the concern troll's favourite tactics is 'tone policing', or trying to detract from an argument by attacking the way it is delivered instead of the actual message.

The sea lion

A sea lion is a troll who continually asks questions or demands evidence for something in order to stifle discussion (think of a toddler going, 'But why? But why? But why?'). Sea-lioning can be particularly pernicious, as it's often hard to tell if someone is genuinely trying to learn or is just wasting your time. When you have finally had enough, the sea lion plays the victim, perhaps trying to justify their behaviour as 'just asking questions' – a phenomenon that Urban Dictionary delightfully defines as 'JAQing off'.

The harasser

Nowadays, the term 'trolling' is colloquially used to describe all manner of online harassment. This can include orchestrated campaigns against people (usually women and minorities) who have different opinions on the most important topics, such as human rights or video games. Tactics include pile-ons of nasty comments, threats of violence and doxing, which means revealing private or identifying information about a person, such as their address or phone number. In some cases, there is little boundary between online and offline harassment.

The troll farm

Trolls at troll farms aren't individual keyboard warriors trying to provoke a response for their own gain; they are employed in groups to produce 'troll' content such as fake news, in a bid to influence political events. A Russian state-backed troll farm called the Internet Research Agency was found to be behind thousands of social media accounts that spread propaganda in the lead-up to the 2016 US elections.

There's no easy solution to dealing with trolls. The old wisdom of 'don't feed the trolls' might work sometimes, but it can also play into harassers' hands by denying their victims a voice. You can block someone or report their account if they overstep a platform or forum's rules – take a screenshot as evidence first – and in cases of actual harassment, it may be appropriate to report it to the police.

Personal attacks, or how to quell your inner troll

There's a common assumption that most online abuse is committed by a small but vocal minority of trolls intent on ruining the internet for everyone else, but Lucas Dixon says that's not always the case. In one study, his team looked at people who made personal attacks within the Wikipedia community.[6] 'We found that, while there are a small number of people who contribute a disproportionately high fraction of the personal attacks on Wikipedia, most personal attacks are not by them,' he says.

In short: it's not just trolls that troll. Dixon calls this the 'bad day hypothesis' – the idea that anyone can have a bad day and then take it out on someone online. Jigsaw is currently working on a tool that aims to predict when a conversation is about to go sour by analysing language patterns, and to advise you to reconsider your contribution before hitting 'send'.

In the meantime, Dixon advises taking a step back to reflect when you feel your inner troll rising. The most obvious sign that a conversation is turning bad, he says, is when someone makes an *ad hominem* attack, which means criticising a person's character instead of their argument. He also warns against assuming ill intent on the part of the other person – which includes accusing them of being a troll who's just trying to derail the conversation. 'That may or may not be true, but if you say it, *you're* going to be helping to derail the conversation,' he points out.

When to leave an argument online

Exercising self-restraint when someone is Wrong On The Internet is a unique emotional struggle, but if any of the following happen, it's time to cut your losses.

- Someone compares something to Hitler or the Nazis (also known as Godwin's Law)
- Someone is anti-Semitic
- A straw man appears
- 'I'm not racist, but. . .'
- Someone purposely mis-genders someone
- There's an *ad hominem* attack
- A swooping generalisation is made
- Someone tries to tone-police you
- 'Just to play devil's advocate. . .'

GLOSSARY

Ad hominem attack

A logical fallacy common in internet arguments, when someone attacks a person delivering an argument instead of the argument itself.

Alt account

A second social media account, usually kept anonymous.

A/S/L

Age/sex/location. An old-school chat room term to ask people to introduce themselves.

Aubergine emoji

A penis.

Backchannel

When you have a real-time conversation with someone on the side of, and in relation to, a larger group chat – for example, WhatsApping a friend one-on-one while also participating in a group chat on the same subject. Also called a side chat.

Belfie

A self-portrait taken from a vantage point such that your most prominent feature is your *derrière*. (A 'bum selfie', if we're being less delicate.)

Blue-ticking

When someone doesn't immediately respond to your message but you can see the two little blue ticks indicating they've read it – thus proving that they're just heartlessly ignoring you. Also called 'being left on read'.

Bot

A fake account run by a software application instead of a human being.

Breadcrumbing

Sending occasional messages to a dating prospect in order to keep them interested without having to invest too much effort or commitment.

Caspering

Coined by presenter Alix Fox in reference to the cartoon 'friendly ghost', caspering is when you cut off communications with a romantic prospect ('ghost' them) but only after sending one last message to politely explain that you're moving on.

Catfish

Someone who pretends to be someone they're not online, often in the context of online dating. A catfish uses a fake identity and images to lure in suitors who otherwise might not be interested.

Concern troll

A troll who poses as an ally but is actually an opponent, and tries to undermine the cause by raising feigned 'concerns' about the issue at hand in order to sow doubt and discord among legitimate supporters.

Cuffing season

The time of year from around November to March when online daters forgo playing the field to instead settle down and snuggle up with someone through the winter.

Deep-liking

The mortifying moment when you're swiping through your crush's years-old Instagram posts and your finger accidentally hits the 'like' button, resulting in them receiving a notification and making you look like the creepy stalker you are.

Doxing

Doxing (also spelled doxxing) is when you publish personal or identifying information about someone online, such as their real name, address, phone number or other details they do not wish to make public. Doxing is often used as a means to harass or threaten people.

DTF

On dating apps: 'down to fuck'.

Duck face

A facial expression characterised by sucking in the cheeks and pouting the lips to make them look fuller, not dissimilar to Zoolander's 'Blue Steel' look. The duck face is common in selfies and frequently paired with the Myspace angle.

Echo chamber

When your'e surrounded by people (online or IRL) who share the same views as you, and so are not exposed to other opinions or perspectives.

Emailing like a CEO

When you respond to emails very fast but with a super-concise response, like a boss.

Fake news

Falsified news stories containing incorrect or made-up information, which are deliberately designed to mislead.

Filter bubble

The phenomenon whereby personalised algorithms show us what they think we want to see.

Finsta

A 'fake' or secondary Instagram account, usually private, where the user posts more personal, unfiltered pictures. (See also: 'Rinsta').

FOMO

'Fear of Missing Out'. That feeling of anxiety when you see everyone else on social media apparently having a better time than you.

Ghosting

When you end a relationship (usually romantic) by suddenly cutting off communication, with no warning or explanation.

Godwin's Law

An internet rule that posits that any argument that goes on long enough will result in someone making a comparison involving Hitler or Nazis. When this happens, the argument is over and that person has lost.

Humblebrag

A social media post whose ostensible humility is a just a thin and ineffective veneer for showing off.

Image macro

A common type of meme that consists of an image overlaid with text, usually to comic effect.

Inbox Zero

An email strategy coined by Merlin Mann by which you triage emails as soon as you read them so as to keep a clean inbox, aka the only way to live.

JAQing off

A trolling tactic in which the troll tries to derail a conversation or influence other people's views by repeatedly asking loaded questions, thus forcing their debate partner onto the back foot under the guise of 'just asking questions'. (Related: Sea lion.)

LTR

Long-term relationship.

Lurker

Someone who regularly reads messages or social media posts but rarely contributes anything themselves.

Mansplaining

When Men Explain Things to You. Mansplaining is when someone (usually a man) explains something to someone else (usually a woman) in a patronising manner, assuming that his conversation partner couldn't possibly know as much about the topic at hand as he does – even if all evidence points to the contrary.

Meme

A piece of internet culture that spreads via adaptation and imitation.

Milkshake Duck

A term to describe someone who is well-loved on social media one moment and falls out of favour the next, after negative details about their past or present behaviour come to light. Coined by Twitter account @PixelatedBoat.

Myspace angle

A selfie taken from a flattering angle which involves holding the phone up and to the side, thus emphasising your eyes and hiding all your chins.

Negging

An emotionally manipulative behaviour whereby someone (usually a man) makes a backhanded compliment to someone else (usually a woman) in order to undermine their confidence.

Netflix and chill

A euphemism for sex.

Nice Guy

A man who believes the only reason he is unsuccessful with women is because he's 'too nice' and 'nice guys finish last'. Endemic on dating apps.

Phubbing

Snubbing a person in real life to instead look at your phone.

Plandid

A photo on social media that is designed to look like a candid shot but is actually clearly staged to look just perfect (a 'planned candid').

Public shaming

When you call out someone's behaviour publicly (i.e. on social media), usually with the intention of damaging their reputation or career.

The Ratio

On Twitter: the ratio between the number of likes and retweets a post receives, and the number of replies it elicits. A tweet that receives many more replies is almost definitely bad.

Reaction gif

A gif, often showing a character's over-the-top facial expression, which is used to express an emotional response.

Regramming

Re-posting someone else's Instagram post.

Reply-allpocalypse

A reply-allpocalypse occurs when someone hits 'reply-all' on an email mistakenly sent to the all-office mailing list, unleashing a flood of subsequent 'reply-alls' that bring productivity to a grinding halt. RIP your inbox.

Revenge porn

Sexually explicit images or videos of someone that are shared without their permission.

Rickrolling

A classic bait-and-switch meme where you trick someone into clicking a link that takes them unexpectedly to the music video of Rick Astley's 80s hit 'Never Gonna Give You Up'.

Rinsta

A 'real' or main Instagram account, where the user posts a curated view of their life for public consumption.

Sea lion

(Not the cute sea mammal.) A specific type of troll who repeatedly asks for evidence or explanations while maintaining an air of utmost civility.

Sexting

Sending sexually explicit messages, including flirtatious texts and saucy images.

Sliding into DMs

The usually-very-awkward transition from speaking to someone through public social media channels to sending them a private message. Not everyone who slides into your DMs is a creep, but many are.

Sparkly unicorn punctuation

When you put ~*~tildes and asterisks~*~ around something to make it look all ~*~sparkly~*~ like an emo teenager on MSN Messenger.

Subgramming

When you post something on Instagram that has a special meaning to one of your followers, without explicitly mentioning them or it.

Subtweeting

When you tweet about someone but either don't mention their name or tag their handle so they don't get alerted to the conversation. It's the Twitter version of bitching behind someone's back.

Thirst trap

A sexy photo (often a mirror selfie) posted on social media explicitly to garner attention and encourage suitors to publicly profess their desire.

Tindstagramming

When you swipe left on someone on Tinder, so they find your profile on Instagram instead and slide into your DMs.

Tone policing

An attempt to shut down or undermine an argument by criticising the way it is delivered rather than its actual content.

Troll

A person who enters an online conversation in bad faith, for example with the intention of disrupting or derailing a conversation, or causing distress to other participants.

Tweetstorm/Twitter thread

A Twitter thread is when you 'thread' multiple tweets together by replying consecutively to each one. A tweetstorm is a Twitter thread that gets out of control, with many threaded tweets pushed out in rapid succession. *Time for some game theory. . .*

Twinstagramming

When two people in a relationship take a picture of the same thing and put it on Instagram.

Typing awareness indicator

The little signifier on messaging apps that shows you someone is in the midst of composing a message while you wait with baited breath to see what they have to say. Sometimes an ellipsis in a bubble, sometimes a message that says '(Name) is typing. . .'

Unicorn

In online dating, a woman prepared to have a no-strings-attached threesome with a heterosexual couple. More commonly found in myth than reality.

Vaguebooking

A social media post, usually on Facebook, in which the poster expresses a negative emotion but neglects to mention the cause of their distress, so that their friends are forced to ask. Usually done for attention.

NOTES

Chapter 1

1. 'Ray Tomlinson, email inventor and selector of @ symbol, dies aged 74' [online], *Guardian*, 2016. Available from: https://www.theguardian.com/technology/2016/mar/07/ray-tomlinson-email-inventor-and-selector-of-symbol-dies-aged-74

2. Mark, G., Iqbal, S. T., Czerwinski, M., Johns, P., Sano, A., 'Email Duration, Batching and Self-Interruption: Patterns of Email Use on Productivity and Stress,' *Proceedings of the 2016 CHI Conference on Human Factors in Computing Systems*, 1717-1728, 2016. Available from: doi: 10.1145/2858036.2858262

3. Jackson, T., Dawson, R. and Wilson, D., 'Case study: Evaluating the Use of an Electronic Messaging System in Business,' *Proceedings of the Conference on Empirical Assessment in Software Engineering*, April 2001, 53-6. Available from: dspace.lboro.ac.uk/2134/488

4. Notopoulos, K., 'I Tried Emailing Like A CEO And Quite Frankly, It Made My Life Better' [online], *Buzzfeed*, 2017. Available from: https://www.buzzfeednews.com/article/katienotopoulos/i-tried-emailing-like-your-boss

5. Wyse, E., ed., (2014), *Debrett's Handbook*, Debrett's Limited, 327

6. Boogaard, K., '4 Valid Reasons You Should Accept Those LinkedIn Requests From Strangers' [online], The Muse. Available from: https://www.themuse.com/advice/4-valid-reasons-you-should-accept-those-linkedin-requests-from-strangers

7. Boogaard, K., 'Here's What Happened When I Accepted Over 300 Random LinkedIn Requests' [online], The Muse. Available from: https://www.themuse.com/advice/heres-what-happened-when-i-accepted-over-300-random-linkedin-requests

Chapter 2

1. Rosenfeld, M. J., Thomas, R. J., 'Searching for a Mate: The Rise of the Internet as a Social Intermediary', *American Sociological Review.* 77(4), pp.523–47, 2012. Available from: doi: 10.1177/0003122412448050

2. Ortega, J., Hergovich, P., 'The Strength of Absent Ties: Social Integration via Online Dating', papers 1709.10478, arXiv.org, 2017, revised September 2018. Available from: arXiv:1709.10478

3. Markowitz, D., 'Undressed: What's the Deal with the Age Gap in Relationships?' [online], *OKCupid Blog*, 2017. Available from: https://theblog.okcupid.com/undressed-whats-the-deal-with-the-age-gap-in-relationships-324a2ca5178

4. Garcia, J. R., et al., 'Sexting among singles in the USA: prevalence of sending, receiving, and sharing sexual messages and images', *Sexual Health,* 2016, 13(5), 428-435. Available from: doi: 10.1071/SH15240

5. Lorenz, T., 'Going 'Instagram Official' is the New Way to Declare Your Relationship Status' [online]. *Medium*, 2017. Available from: https://medium.com/@taylorlorenz/going-instagram-official-is-the-new-way-to-declare-your-relationship-status-a64f89f7fadc

6. Thompson, R., 'My Hinge Match Invited Me to Dinner and Blocked Me as I Waited For Our Table' [online], *Mashable,* 2018. Available from: https://mashable.com/article/online-dating-blocked-stood-up/?europe=true#ML8sUuzjlqqf

7. Hendricks, S., '17 Ghosting Stories That Will Make You Want to Give Up Dating Forever' [online], *Insider,* 2018. Available from: https://www.thisisinsider.com/worst-ghosting-stories-real-people-twitter-2018-5

Chapter 3

1. Mai, L. M., Freudenthaler, R., Schneider, F. M., Vorderer, P., "I know you've seen it!' Individual and social factors for users' chatting behavior on Facebook', *Computers in Human Behavior.* 49, August 2015, 296–302. Available from: doi: 10.1016/j.chb.2015.01.074

2. Ashmore, J., 'Labour MP apologises after 'bollocks position' WhatsApp message' [online], *Politics Home.* Available from: https://www.politicshome.com/news/uk/political-parties/labour-party/news/82828/labour-mp-apologises-after-bollocks-position

3. Wall, H. J., Kaye, L. K., Malone, S. A., 'An Exploration of Psychological Factors on Emoticon Usage and Implications for Judgement Accuracy', *Computers in Human Behavior,* 62, September 2016, 70–78. Available from: doi: 10.1016/j.chb.2016.03.040

4. Rossignol, J., 'Apple Says 'Face With Tears of Joy' is Most Popular Emoji in United States Among English Speakers' [online], *MacRumors,* 2017. Available from: https://www.macrumors.com/2017/11/03/face-with-tears-of-joy-most-popular-emoji/

5. Adamic, L., Develin, M., Weinsberg, U., 'The Not-So-Universal Language of Laughter' [online], *Facebook*

Research, 2015/ Available from: https://research.fb.com/the-not-so-universal-language-of-laughter/

Chapter 4

1. Zhong, C., Chang, H.W., Karamshuk, D., Lee, D. & Sastry, N., 'Wearing many (social) hats: How different are your different social network personae?', *Proceedings of the 11th International Conference on Web and Social Media*, AAAI press, 2017, 397-406.
2. Dunbar, R.I.M., 'The Anatomy of Friendship', *Trends in Cognitive Sciences* [online], 22(1), 32–51. Available from: doi: 10.1016/j.tics.2017.10.004
3. Bakhshi, S., Shamma, D.A., Gilbert, E., 'Faces Engage Us: Photos with Faces Attract More Likes and Comments on Instagram,' *Proceedings of the SIGCHI Conference on Human Factors in Computing Systems*, [online], 2014, 965–974. Available from: doi: 10.1145/2556288.2557403
4. Levinson, A.H., 'Men, Please Stop Manthreading' [online], *Gizmodo*, 2016. Available from: https://gizmodo.com/men-please-stop-manthreading-1790036387
5. Reuters Institute for the Study of Journalism, 'Digital News Report 2018' [online]. *Digital News Report*, 2018. Available from: http://www.digitalnewsreport.org/
6. Wulczyn, E., Thain, N., Dixon, L., 'Ex Machina: Personal Attacks Seen at Scale', *WWW '17 Proceedings of the 26th International Conference on World Wide Web* [online], 2017, 1391–1399. Available from: doi: 10.1145/3038912.3052591

INDEX